T0244464

THE PREACHER'S HEBREW/GREEK COMPANION SERIES

General Editor / Old Testament Editor

JONATHAN G. KLINE, PhD

Senior Editor
Hendrickson Publishers

New Testament Editor

SEAN M. MCDONOUGH, PhD

Professor of New Testament
Gordon-Conwell Theological Seminary

The Preacher's Greek Companion Series

Colossians

THE PREACHER'S GREEK COMPANION TO

Colossians

A Selective Commentary for
Meditation and Sermon Preparation

Haley Jacob

HENDRICKSON
ACADEMIC

an imprint of Hendrickson Publishing Group

The Preacher's Greek Companion to Colossians:
A Selective Commentary for Meditation and Sermon Preparation

© 2024 by Hendrickson Publishers

Published by Hendrickson Academic
Hendrickson Publishers, LLC
P. O. Box 3473
Peabody, Massachusetts 01961-3473
www.hendricksonpublishers.com

ISBN 978-1-68307-350-5

Printed in the United States of America

First Printing — December 2024

CONTENTS

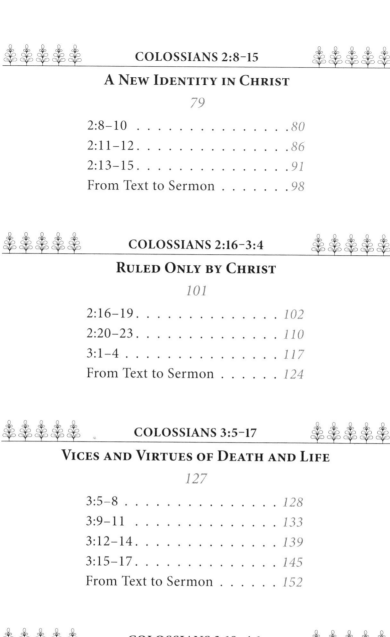

COLOSSIANS 4:2–18

Exhortations and Greetings

175

Overview

Like many preachers, you may wish you could use the biblical languages in your sermon preparation, but the task seems daunting. Perhaps you lack confidence in your language skills—especially if it's been a long time since you studied Greek or Hebrew—and when you turn to technical commentaries, you feel overwhelmed. Or perhaps you simply don't have the time to do the laborious work of digging into the original-language texts. To help you overcome these challenges, we designed this series, the Preacher's Greek Companion (as well as its Old Testament counterpart series, the Preacher's Hebrew Companion). In collaboration with the series authors, our goal as series editors is to gently guide you, the busy preacher, through the Greek text of select biblical passages in a way that will empower you to integrate original-language exegesis and homiletics. Our prayer is that you will find this book and the other volumes in this series spiritually and intellectually encouraging as well as pleasant to use. We hope your use of the series will make your sermon preparation a more profound and satisfying process and will invigorate your preaching.

Structure

Each volume in this series includes the following three features for a given biblical book (or portion of a book):

- ⚘ **a curated selection of passages** we believe many preachers would likely choose to preach on from the biblical book (or portion of the book) in question; **or, for shorter biblical books, the entire book**, broken up into manageable passages

- ⚘ all the basic **lexical and grammatical tools** you need (whatever your Greek skill level may be) **to work through and meditate on the Greek text** of these passages in a way that strengthens your sermon preparation and empowers you to preach more effectively

- ⚘ **succinct, select comments** intended to help you responsibly and effectively bridge the gap between reading the Greek text and delivering a sermon on it

The Preacher's Greek Companion is not a traditional commentary series, as is reflected in its title and subtitle: "*Companion*" (not "*Commentary*") and "*Selected* Passages for *Meditation* and *Sermon Preparation*." That is, we conceived this series as a *supplement* to the wealth of fine commentaries that already exist, not as a replacement for any of them. We recommend using this series alongside traditional commentaries, which by design include helpful information that is not covered in ours.

The Selection of Passages

Each volume in the Preacher's Greek Companion series provides the Greek text of **approximately ten to twelve passages** from a particular biblical book (or portion thereof):

 In addition to having expertise in Greek and exegesis, our series authors typically have extensive preaching experience or are full-time preachers by vocation. Unless the biblical book in question is short enough to be included in full, they chose **passages** they think **preachers would most likely desire to preach**. In order to encourage preaching through the biblical book in an "expository" rather than a thematic manner, these passages are presented in canonical order. That said, for longer books (such as Isaiah or Matthew), we encouraged authors to choose passages that highlight or represent important themes found in the book; for such books, however, the chosen passages are still presented in canonical order. The curated, limited number of passages in each series volume allows you, if you wish, to use the passages as the basis for a "ready-made" sermon series of whatever length suits your schedule (e.g., for a series consisting of, say, four, seven, ten, or twelve sermons). Alternatively, you might choose to preach a series using some of the passages in a volume and then supplement these with passages from the biblical book in question that are not found in the volume.

 The aims of the series guided our decisions about passage length. On the one hand, we encouraged authors to choose **passages that are not too long**, so that the portions of text won't be daunting to you if your Greek skills are rudimentary; nor do we want you to be overwhelmed by wading through dozens of verses in Greek. For this reason, our ideal length for most passages has been approximately ten verses. On the other hand, in order to do justice to the natural boundaries of longer passages, we have taken care not to artificially truncate such texts. Consider, for example, the account of the crossing of the Red Sea (Exod 14–15) or the story of the raising of Lazarus (John 11). Although these texts are far too long to be included in full in a volume in this series, each constituent part of these texts is vital to understanding their narrative development and message. For such passages, we asked authors to focus—as a preacher might typically do when delivering a sermon on a lengthy passage—on what they consider to be the most salient verses from the passage. Accordingly, we have provided the Greek text for only these verses, with the author summarizing the other verses (in English).

🌱 Finally, when authors deemed it helpful (especially for longer biblical books), they have indicated, on the first page devoted to each passage, the **larger literary unit to which the passage belongs**,[1] thus helping you see the passage in question as part of a larger whole rather than as an isolated pericope. In cases where this larger literary context is indicated, we encourage you to pick up a Bible and read and dwell on this context while using this volume to work through the passage.

The Presentation of Each Passage

This volume helps you work through each passage it contains by presenting the Greek text of the passage along with the lexical and grammatical information you need in order to dig into this original-language text. Designed to be highly accessible, this format is intended (1) to enable you to work through the text in manageable chunks and according to your abilities, regardless of your skill level in Greek; (2) to simultaneously facilitate both study and devotion; and (3) in conjunction with the author's commentary, to help you bridge the gap, as easily and seamlessly as possible, between the original-language text and preaching.

More specifically, this volume contains the following five sections for each passage:

🌱 A **brief introduction** to the passage—typically comprising only a few sentences—is included in order to set the stage for the passage and highlight its important themes.

🌱 For ease of reading and to encourage you to slow down and contemplate the text, the passage is typically divided into subunits. For each of these subunits, we provide the **Greek text** of each clause or phrase, along with **transliteration** (as a pronunciation help for those whose Greek is at a rudimentary level) and the author's **translation**.[2]

---

1. Occasionally, such a literary unit is coterminous with the passage itself.
2. The Greek text used in this series is that of the 1885 Westcott-Hort edition of the New Testament, as printed in B. F. Westcott and F. J. A. Hort, *The Greek New Testament,*

Next, each clause or phrase from the subunit is presented in an interlinear fashion, notably with **a contextual gloss (or multiple contextual glosses) and parsing for each word**.[3] For example:

3a	**Εὐχαριστῶ τῷ θεῷ μου**		
	I give thanks to my God		
Εὐχαριστῶ εὐχαριστέω	I am giving thanks/ give thanks *Eu·cha·ri·stō*	PRES ACT IND 1ST SG	verb
τῷ ὁ	to the *tō*	DAT SG MASC	article
θεῷ θεός	(to) God *the·ō*	DAT SG MASC	noun
μου ἐγώ	of me/my *mou*	1ST GEN SG	personal pron

This formatting allows you to easily analyze each word in the clause or phrase (by helping you on the level of semantics and morphology) and to perceive how the words work together as a whole (by helping you on the level of syntax).

 A key feature of each volume in this series is the inclusion of **concise comments** to accompany some clauses and phrases. These have two primary goals: (1) to enable you to understand and exegete the text more deeply than might be possible from reading it in English, and (2) to equip you with insights into the original-language text that will be of direct value for your preaching. To help you focus and not become overwhelmed with too much information, we encouraged our authors to comment only on those clauses and phrases for which they thought doing so would accomplish these two goals. In addition, because the volumes in this series are not only language aids but—ultimately and more importantly—preaching aids, we asked authors to highlight those features in the Greek text that bring out key themes, rhetorical and theological emphasis, narrative de-

---

with *Expanded Dictionary* (Peabody, MA: Hendrickson Publishers, 2008). For interested readers, text-critical variants for the passages included in the present volume are presented at the end of the volume.

3. The parsings are derived from an unpublished database created by Mark House and Maurice Robinson for Hendrickson Publishers. The glosses are the author's own, though sometimes they are based on glosses from the aforementioned database. The glosses intentionally err on the "literal" end of the spectrum, in order to help you apprehend the basic meaning(s) of each word in context.

velopment, character development, connections with other biblical texts, and the like. Although noting various other features in the Greek text may have been intrinsically interesting from a grammatical perspective or helpful for strengthening your language skills, authors have generally refrained from commenting on such features when doing so would not be likely to aid you in moving from text to sermon in any substantial way.[4] In short, an author's brief, select comments are intended—in conjunction with the volume's language aids—to provide you both with *focus* and with *space* to slow down, meditate, wonder, and mature in your understanding and experience of the text, as you form your own judgments on it and prepare to proclaim the divine word to your hearers. The author's comments are not intended to circumscribe the possible interpretive options with one single answer (especially for texts whose interpretation is the particular subject of debate among Christian believers). Rather, they are meant to stimulate your thinking, to help you see features of the text (and connections with other texts) that you may not have perceived before, and to prompt you to ask questions that may not have previously occurred to you.

 Each passage ends with a brief section titled **"From Text to Sermon,"** in which our authors, building on their comments, suggest ways you can move from working through the Greek text to the task of homiletics, highlighting potential points of emphasis or particular insights you may wish to share with your audience. In this way, the authors provide you with possible ways to bring the text to life for your audience (e.g., types of illustrations you might use). Because individual preachers (and each of our series authors) bring their own particular skills, perspectives, backgrounds, and oratorical approaches to bear on the homiletical task, and because every biblical text has its own unique features, we encouraged our authors to structure the "From Text to Sermon" section as a free-form series of short paragraphs whose content and emphases are guided by their own personal judgment about what is most helpful for a variety of preachers in different places, cultures, and times. The remarks in this section are always grouped according to rubrics (in the form of inline

---

4. Another way we have kept the presentation streamlined and uncluttered, so that you can achieve maximum focus, is by intentionally keeping source citations to a minimum. Authors' comments on a given passage are the fruit of their scholarly research on the passage, their personal reflection on it, and their experience preaching and teaching it. They cite secondary sources only when they draw a specific insight from one particular source or wish to point you to a particularly helpful resource for further reading. As stated above, we naturally encourage you to also use traditional commentaries (which typically provide more documentation) in your study and sermon preparation.

headers); but rather than restrict authors with a "one-size-fits-all" set of rubrics, we allowed them to create their own rubrics and even, if helpful, to vary these rubrics across passages within their volume in light of the unique features and emphases of each passage.[5] We view the resulting diversity of approaches and emphases across this series (and even within a given volume) as a strength, and we hope this aspect of the series will encourage you to use your own judgment about how to preach each passage in a way that best suits you and your listeners, being sensitive to the promptings and guidance of the Spirit of God.

Audience and Theological Perspective

Since our hope is that many different kinds of people will find the volumes in this series useful, we have designed the Preacher's Greek Companion to be helpful to a broad spectrum of Christian preachers:

- 🌱 Our intention is that the series will be **useful and accessible to a large and diverse group of preachers serving a variety of communities throughout the world**. For this reason, we encouraged authors to exercise sensitivity and broad-mindedness in their comments and particularly when writing the "From Text to Sermon" section, in which they could run the risk of being too culturally specific. In particular, we asked authors that any sermon illustrations they included in this section generally be as universal as possible or that, instead of providing specific illustrations, they point to themes from the passage you may wish to illustrate in one way or another. That said, because specificity is essential for good communication, we also allowed authors to suggest—when they deemed it particularly helpful—concrete, culturally specific examples as springboards to help you think about examples that will be relevant for your own context.

- 🌱 We asked our authors to express any **theological perspectives** in a way that is **consistent with the beliefs stated in the Apostles' Creed**. Because this series aims to meet the needs of Christian preachers of various theological viewpoints, we encouraged a diversity of theological perspectives within these bounds across the volumes in the series. In addition, because the series has a joint focus on exegesis (close attention to what a specific text says) and homiletics (how to preach said text), we advised authors

---

5. That said, we suggested the following possible rubrics to authors as starting points to consider: theological themes, themes for application and illustration, integrating the broader historical and literary context, learning from the language, and (as deemed helpful and not reductionistic) "the big idea" of the passage.

when making any theological comments to let these flow naturally from the text at hand, rather than using the text as a springboard to discuss issues that would more properly fall under the rubric of systematic theology. Although we asked authors to avoid reading any given passage through the lens of a theological system grounded in other biblical texts, we also strongly encouraged them to discuss allusions to other biblical passages or other innerbiblical literary connections if they felt that doing so would help you understand the message of the text at hand and know how to preach it more effectively.

Acknowledgments

We would like to offer our heartfelt gratitude to the following individuals, who have played a central role in the creation of this series:

- Arley Kangas, Marco Resendes, and Tyler Comer, for their excellent work on various aspects of the making of these volumes, especially transliterating, proofreading, and generating the indexes.

- Phil Frank, for his expert typesetting and for patiently working with us, in our capacity as series editors, to achieve the desired formatting and aesthetic for these volumes.

- The series authors, for joining us in this unique project and for sharing our vision and lending their considerable skills to the task. These volumes are the result of a fruitful collaboration between the Hendrickson team and the series authors (with both parties contributing to the content). We are truly grateful for the opportunity to have worked on this project together.

All of us—the series editors, the series authors, and the team at Hendrickson—pray that the volume you now hold in your hands will empower and encourage you to work through the Greek text of the Bible in order to deepen your sermon preparation and strengthen your proclamation of the word of God. We nurture a deep respect and appreciation for the challenging work that you as a preacher do on the "front lines," and we recognize the many challenges (logistical, mental, emotional, spiritual, and more) that you encounter on a weekly, indeed a daily, basis. We are honored to come alongside you and support you in your important labors, and we pray that your use of this book will bear much fruit for the kingdom of God.

JONATHAN G. KLINE
SEAN M. MCDONOUGH

.

If I had to choose just one of Paul's epistles that I thought had the power to transform Christianity in the twenty-first century, I would choose Colossians. After a close reading, you begin to realize that the cultural and theological questions that plagued the Colossian Christians in the first century are, in fact, quite like those that plague Christians in the twenty-first century: questions of identity, culture, gospel, salvation, and lifestyle. Colossians is about new life in Christ and how that impacts our relationships with ourselves, our fellow Christians, those within our house, and even the non-Christians in our midst. Indeed, Colossians raises important questions for every twenty-first century Christian, everywhere.

And yet I don't remember the last time I heard a sermon on Colossians.

The theological weightiness, particularly of the first three chapters, makes it feel quite daunting. For those who attempt to read the letter in the original Greek, the long, long, long, seemingly unending sentences make it difficult to even follow Paul's points, let alone try to make theological sense of them and then preach about them! And then, isn't it easier just to preach about the stories of Jesus from the Gospels or a classic verse or two from Romans? But here's the deal: Colossians is a letter for the twenty-first century, one churches today desperately need to hear. And with the help of this volume and other traditional commentaries, it is both discernable and preachable.

Here are just a few of the significant truths that believers today need to hear from Colossians: Christians are called to live lives *worthy* of the Lord; Christians were formerly enemies of God, fighting on behalf of the kingdom of darkness (it sounds like a video game!); Jesus is the God of Gen 1; God *has* reconciled *all things* to himself; some people within the church have their own self-determined religious obligations that they are actively trying to persuade others to follow; believers have already died once; the good news of the gospel is that, through the cross, Jesus *both* made possible the forgiveness of sins *and* triumphed over evil powers at work in the world; the believer's truest existence is *in* Christ *in* heaven; the Christian lifestyle "behind closed doors" ought to demonstrate a believer's life in Christ; unity within the church is not optional; proclaiming the whole gospel to non-Christians is also not optional and, for those in cultures particularly hostile toward Christianity, this may land them in prison. Many more relevant truths could be mentioned. Needless to say, there are a few things in Colossians that the church today would do well to dwell on.

For those preaching on this text who are relatively unfamiliar with some of the current conversations taking place within Pauline scholarship, let me mention two theological themes that will be highlighted quite frequently throughout this commentary. If either of these Pauline emphases is not understood, the letter itself will be indiscernible.

The first is the idea of participation or unity in Christ. I regularly like to ask my students, "What is the most underappreciated word in Paul's letters?" The answer, which they never guess, is "in." Throughout the Pauline corpus, Paul describes believers as being "in Christ" over 160 times. In doing so, he describes a whole gamut of truths about the believer's identity, the most fundamental of which is the idea that a believer's identity is found *in Christ*. What is true of Christ is true of the believer. If Christ is a child of God, then the believer is a child of God *in Christ*. If Christ is declared justified, then the believer is declared justified, because his or her identity is *in Christ*. If Christ is at the right hand of God, then the believer, in his or her truest, most fundamental, most genuine existence, is also at the right hand of God *in Christ*. This idea of being in Christ is foundational to Paul's message to the church in Colossae. I highly suggest that anyone preaching on the text spend a few moments reading the entry on "In Christ" in the second edition of the *Dictionary of Paul and His Letters* (2023). It is a beautiful introduction by a wonderful New Testament scholar named Michael Gorman to the highly significant and rather complex topic of participation or union in Christ.

The second emphasis that is essential to understanding the letter of Colossians is what scholars refer to as Paul's apocalyptic theology. In comparison to the theme of union in Christ, this theological theme is, unfortunately, both less straightforward in the letter itself (and, indeed in the entire Pauline corpus), and requires a broader background knowledge in terms of the theological culture from which it stemmed in Paul's first century Jewish world. The basic idea is that for Paul and many of his contemporaries the spiritual world involved more than just God. It included evil forces that Paul refers to by various names, such as Flesh, Satan, Sin, Death, rulers of this age, kingdom of darkness, etc. These evil forces are responsible for the brokenness of the good, created order that we read about in Gen 1. They are also responsible for enslaving people to evil. Until Jesus' death on the cross, these powers ruled over the earth. At the cross, Paul will say in Col 2:15, Jesus triumphed over them. We now await Christ's return and their final defeat. Until then, we must recognize that the war continues and that these same evil forces will continue to destroy, betray, and enslave. For this reason, Paul writes that we should "put on the full armor of God, so that you can take your stand against the devil's schemes. For our struggle is not against flesh and blood, but against the rulers, against the authorities, against the powers of this dark world and against the spiritual forces of evil in the heavenly realms" (Eph 6:11–12 NIV). Throughout this volume, words like sin, flesh, and death will not generally be capitalized unless they are referring to evil spiritual forces. When these words do occur, the reader is encouraged to consider whether they imply evil spiritual forces, i.e., "Flesh" or "Sin," or whether they imply "flesh" or "sin" as they are traditionally understood.

In the midst of this spiritual battle, God *revealed* himself in the birth, life, death, resurrection, and ascension of Jesus the Messiah. This revelation is the apocalyptic aspect of Paul's theology, the term "apocalypse" coming from the Greek ἀποκάλυψις ("unveiling/revelation"). In Jesus, God revealed his true power, redeemed his creation, brought forgiveness to his people, and launched the new creation—a new creation untouched by evil. Much more can and should be said on this topic. Again, I highly encourage you to look at the entry titled "Apocalyptic Paul" written by Jamie Davies in the second edition of the *Dictionary of Paul and His Letters* (2023). Davies does an excellent job walking the reader through the history of the theological conversation, the nuances of the conversation, and the various ways in which these apocalyptic emphases appear in Paul's epistles.

When Jonathan Kline and Sean McDonough invited me to join this series in June 2020, I had a nine-month-old baby and was pregnant with my second. There would be no time for sleep over the next couple of years, let alone freedom to work on a fun project such as this. To my surprise, when I said "yes" but only if they could wait three years, they said "great"! Now, four years later, I am grateful to both of them—to Jonathan for his patience and understanding as I've navigated the many deadlines and sleepless nights over the last few years, and to Sean for introducing me to the beautiful complexities of Colossians while a student at GCTS. Sean gave me a well-deserved B on a paper and an A- in that course, only to invite me to write this commentary nearly fifteen years later. Thanks to him, I now have a lovely anecdote to share with my students about the (un)importance of grades, and a gentle reminder that the God we serve is a God of grace and humor!

LIST OF ABBREVIATIONS

1ST	first person	indef	indefinite
2ND	second person	INF	infinitive
3RD	third person	interr	interrogative
ACC	accusative	MASC	masculine
ACT	active	MID	middle
adj	adjective	NEUT	neuter
adv	adverb	NOM	nominative
AOR	aorist	num	numerical
comp	comparative	OPT	optative
cond	conditional	PASS	passive
conj	conjunction	PERF	perfect
DAT	dative	PL	plural
demonstr	demonstrative	prep	preposition
FEM	feminine	PRES	present
FUT	future	pron	pronoun
GEN	genitive	PTCP	participle
Heb	Hebrew	SG	singular
IMPF	imperfect	SUBJ	subjunctive
IMPV	imperative	translit	transliteration
IND	indicative	VOC	vocative

NOTE: All Old Testament verse numbers in this volume refer to the Hebrew text. Where the English verse numbering differs, it is listed in brackets following the Hebrew numbering, without any special notation. When the Septuagint (i.e., Greek) version of an Old Testament text is cited and the verse numbering differs from that of the Hebrew text, the Greek reference is listed in brackets following the Hebrew reference, accompanied by the notation "LXX".

THANKSGIVING AND PRAYER

Paul's letter to the Colossians begins with his thanksgiving for their acceptance and proclamation of the gospel, demonstrated in their faith in Christ and their love for one another. They heard the gospel as a result of the ministry of Epaphras, who was presumably sent as a representative of Paul and Timothy. Paul prays for the Colossian Christians to be able to live lives worthy of the Lord—lives that demonstrate their redemption and participation in the kingdom of the Son of God.

1a

Παῦλος ἀπόστολος Χριστοῦ Ἰησοῦ

Paulos apostolos Christou Iēsou

Paul, an apostle of Christ Jesus,

1b

διὰ θελήματος θεοῦ

dia thelēmatos theou

through the will of God,

1c

καὶ Τιμόθεος ὁ ἀδελφὸς

kai Timotheos ho adelphos

and Timothy our brother,

2a

τοῖς ἐν Κολοσσαῖς ἁγίοις

tois en Kolossais hagiois

to the saints in Colossae,

2b

καὶ πιστοῖς ἀδελφοῖς ἐν Χριστῷ·

kai pistois adelphois en Christō;

the faithful brothers and sisters in Christ.

2c

χάρις ὑμῖν καὶ εἰρήνη

charis hymin kai eirēnē

Grace and peace to you

2d

ἀπὸ θεοῦ πατρὸς ἡμῶν.

apo theou patros hēmon.

from God our father.

3-8

[SUMMARIZED BELOW]

Παῦλος ἀπόστολος Χριστοῦ Ἰησοῦ

Paul, an apostle of Christ Jesus,

Παῦλος Παῦλος	Paul *Pau·los*	NOM SG MASC	noun
ἀπόστολος ἀπόστολος	apostle *a·po·sto·los*	NOM SG MASC	noun
Χριστοῦ Χριστός	of Christ *Chri·stou*	GEN SG MASC	noun
Ἰησοῦ Ἰησοῦς	(of) Jesus *I·ē·sou*	GEN SG MASC	noun

διὰ θελήματος θεοῦ

through the will of God,

διὰ διά	through/because of *di·a*	---	prep
θελήματος θέλημα	will *the·lē·ma·tos*	GEN SG NEUT	noun
θεοῦ θεός	of God *the·ou*	GEN SG MASC	noun

καὶ Τιμόθεος ὁ ἀδελφὸς

and Timothy our brother,

καὶ καί	and *kai*	---	conj
Τιμόθεος Τιμόθεος	Timothy *Ti·mo·the·os*	NOM SG MASC	noun
ὁ ὁ	the *ho*	NOM SG MASC	article
ἀδελφὸς ἀδελφός	brother *a·del·phos*	NOM SG MASC	noun

That Paul writes "the brother" rather than the expected "our brother" may indicate the magnitude of Timothy's reputation among the churches in and around Colossae.

2a	**τοῖς ἐν Κολοσσαῖς ἁγίοις**		
	to the saints in Colossae,		
τοῖς	to the (ones)	DAT PL MASC	article
ὁ	*tois*		
ἐν	in	---	prep
ἐν	*en*		
Κολοσσαῖς	Colossae	DAT PL FEM	noun
Κολοσσαί	*Ko·los·sais*		
ἁγίοις	saints/holy ones	DAT PL MASC	adj
ἅγιος	*ha·gi·ois*		

2b	**καὶ πιστοῖς ἀδελφοῖς ἐν Χριστῷ·**		
	the faithful brothers and sisters in Christ.		
καὶ	and	---	conj
καί	*kai*		
πιστοῖς	to faithful (ones)	DAT PL MASC	adj
πιστός	*pi·stois*		
ἀδελφοῖς	to brothers	DAT PL MASC	noun
ἀδελφός	*a·del·phois*		
ἐν	in	---	prep
ἐν	*en*		
Χριστῷ	Christ	DAT SG MASC	noun
Χριστός	*Chri·stō*		

Paul begins his letter by addressing the recipients as those who are **ἐν Χριστῷ** ("in Christ"), reminding them of the only identity that ultimately matters. Understanding the importance of this language for Paul is critical to understanding his letter to the Colossians. See the overview of Paul's language concerning "participation in Christ" in the "Author's Introduction" at the beginning of this volume.

2c	**χάρις ὑμῖν καὶ εἰρήνη**		
	Grace and peace to you		
χάρις	grace	NOM SG FEM	noun
χάρις	*cha·ris*		
ὑμῖν	to you (all)	2ND DAT PL	personal
σύ	*hy·min*		pron

καὶ καί	and *kai*	- - -	conj
εἰρήνη εἰρήνη	peace *ei·rē·nē*	NOM SG FEM	noun

Paul's use of **εἰρήνη** ("peace") here does not refer to some form of inner tranquility. It denotes, rather, the sense of rightness, justness, or harmony that ought to exist between God and the created order, including humanity. It thus corresponds to the Hebrew concept of peace, or shalom, seen in the broader redemption narrative begun in Genesis. Peace in this sense will be the ultimate form of redemption within Paul's apocalyptic framework; where there is peace, there is no evil or brokenness of relationships. See Col 1:20; 3:15.

2d	**ἀπὸ θεοῦ πατρὸς ἡμῶν.**		
	from God our father.		
ἀπὸ ἀπό	from *a·po*	- - -	prep
θεοῦ θεός	God *the·ou*	GEN SG MASC	noun
πατρὸς πατήρ	father *pa·tros*	GEN SG MASC	noun
ἡμῶν ἐγώ	of us/our *hē·mon*	1ST GEN PL	personal pron

1:3–8	**SUMMARY**

Jesus' command to "love God and love your neighbor" had taken root among the Colossians. In 1:3–8, Paul praises them for their faith in the gospel and their love for one another. The gospel has borne fruit and has grown among them since the day they first heard it from Epaphras (cf. the comments on Col 1:10).

9a
Διὰ τοῦτο καὶ ἡμεῖς,

Dia touto kai hēmeis,

That is why,

9b
ἀφ᾽ ἧς ἡμέρας ἠκούσαμεν,

aph' hēs hēmeras ēkousamen,

from the day we heard it,

9c
οὐ παυόμεθα ὑπὲρ ὑμῶν προσευχόμενοι

ou pauometha hyper hymōn proseuchomenoi

we have not stopped praying for you.

9d
καὶ αἰτούμενοι ἵνα πληρωθῆτε

kai aitoumenoi hina plērōthēte

τὴν ἐπίγνωσιν τοῦ θελήματος αὐτοῦ

tēn epignōsin tou thelēmatos autou

We ask that you may be filled with the knowledge of his will

9e
ἐν πάσῃ σοφίᾳ καὶ συνέσει πνευματικῇ,

en pasē sophia kai synesei pneumatikē,

through all the wisdom and understanding that the Spirit gives,

10a
περιπατῆσαι ἀξίως τοῦ κυρίου

peripatēsai axiōs tou kyriou

so that you may live in a manner worthy of the Lord,

10b
εἰς πᾶσαν ἀρεσκίαν

eis pasan areskian

pleasing him in every way,

10c
ἐν παντὶ ἔργῳ ἀγαθῷ καρποφοροῦντες

en panti ergō agathō karpophorountes

bearing fruit in every good work

10d

καὶ αὐξανόμενοι τῇ ἐπιγνώσει τοῦ θεοῦ,

kai auxanomenoi tē epignōsei tou theou,

and growing in the knowledge of God;

11a

ἐν πάσῃ δυνάμει δυναμούμενοι

en pasē dynamei dynamoumenoi

being equipped with all power

11b

κατὰ τὸ κράτος τῆς δόξης αὐτοῦ

kata to kratos tēs doxēs autou

by his glorious might,

11c

εἰς πᾶσαν ὑπομονὴν καὶ μακροθυμίαν.

eis pasan hypomonēn kai makrothymian.

so that you might have endurance and patience,

11d–12a

Μετὰ χαρᾶς εὐχαριστοῦντες

Meta charas eucharistountes

τῷ πατρὶ τῷ ἱκανώσαντι ὑμᾶς

tō patri tō hikanōsanti hymas

giving joyful thanks to the Father, who has qualified you

12b

εἰς τὴν μερίδα τοῦ κλήρου τῶν ἁγίων ἐν τῷ φωτί,

eis tēn merida tou klērou tōn hagiōn en tō phōti,

to share in the inheritance of the saints in the kingdom of light.

13a

ὃς ἐρύσατο ἡμᾶς ἐκ τῆς ἐξουσίας τοῦ σκότους

hos erysato hēmas ek tēs exousias tou skotous

He has rescued us from the dominion of darkness

13b

καὶ μετέστησεν εἰς τὴν βασιλείαν

kai metestēsen eis tēn basileian

τοῦ υἱοῦ τῆς ἀγάπης αὐτοῦ,

tou huiou tēs agapēs autou,

and transferred us into the kingdom of the Son he loves,

ἐν ᾧ ἔχομεν τὴν ἀπολύτρωσιν,

en hō echomen tēn apolytrōsin,

in whom we have redemption,

τὴν ἄφεσιν τῶν ἁμαρτιῶν·

tēn aphesin tōn hamartiōn;

the freedom from sins.

9a	Διὰ τοῦτο καὶ ἡμεῖς,		
	That is why,		
Διὰ διά	on account of/because of *Di·a*	---	prep
τοῦτο οὗτος	this *tou·to*	ACC SG NEUT	demonstr pron
καὶ καί	and/also *kai*	---	conj
ἡμεῖς ἐγώ	we *hē·meis*	1ST NOM PL	personal pron

The **ἡμεῖς** ("we") here is the subject of **ἠκούσαμεν** ("we heard") in the following clause.

9b	ἀφ᾽ ἧς ἡμέρας ἠκούσαμεν,		
	from the day we heard it,		
ἀφ᾽ ἀπό	from *aph'*	---	prep
ἧς ὅς	which *hēs*	GEN SG FEM	relative pron
ἡμέρας ἡμέρα	day *hē·me·ras*	GEN SG FEM	noun
ἠκούσαμεν ἀκούω	we heard *ē·kou·sa·men*	AOR ACT IND 1ST PL	verb

οὐ παυόμεθα ὑπὲρ ὑμῶν προσευχόμενοι

we have not stopped praying for you.

Greek	English	Parsing	Type
οὐ οὐ	not *ou*	---	particle
παυόμεθα παύω	we cease *pau·o·me·tha*	PRES MID IND 1ST PL	verb
ὑπὲρ ὑπέρ	on behalf of/for *hy·per*	---	prep
ὑμῶν σύ	you (all) *hy·mōn*	2ND GEN PL	personal pron
προσευχόμενοι προσεύχομαι	praying *pros·eu·cho·me·noi*	PRES MID PTCP NOM PL MASC	verb

Notice that vv. 9–14 constitute one continuous sentence. While keeping the translation as one long sentence might sound beautiful and rich, it becomes difficult for many listeners or readers to grasp which points are primary and which are secondary. Paul's point becomes more accessible to listeners today if the clauses are broken into shorter sentences.

καὶ αἰτούμενοι ἵνα πληρωθῆτε
τὴν ἐπίγνωσιν τοῦ θελήματος αὐτοῦ

We ask that you may be filled with the knowledge of his will

Greek	English	Parsing	Type
καὶ καί	and *kai*	---	conj
αἰτούμενοι αἰτέω	asking/requesting *ai·tou·me·noi*	PRES MID PTCP NOM PL MASC	verb
ἵνα ἵνα	that *hi·na*	---	conj
πληρωθῆτε πληρόω	you might be filled with *plē·rō·thē·te*	AOR PASS SUBJ 2ND PL	verb
τὴν ὁ	the *tēn*	ACC SG FEM	article
ἐπίγνωσιν ἐπίγνωσις	knowledge *e·pi·gnō·sin*	ACC SG FEM	noun
τοῦ ὁ	of the *tou*	GEN SG NEUT	article
θελήματος θέλημα	(of) will *the·lē·ma·tos*	GEN SG NEUT	noun
αὐτοῦ αὐτός	of him/his *au·tou*	GEN SG MASC	personal pron

Paul will refer to **ἐπίγνωσις** ("knowledge") four times in Colossians (1:9, 10; 2:2; 3:10). In each case, **ἐπίγνωσις** does not refer primarily to an intellectual knowledge but rather to a spiritual or practical knowledge of God himself, who the source of true knowledge. It is a knowledge that becomes synonymous with **σοφία** ("wisdom") and **συνέσει πνευματικῇ** ("spiritual understanding") in the next clause. It is the sort of knowledge that leads to or even assumes personal transformation as a result of it, as Paul implies in the next verse. Paul is not suggesting that everyone must understand Greek or Hebrew or have a seminary education but that the most important knowledge is already available to everyone in Christ.

9e	**ἐν πάσῃ σοφίᾳ καὶ συνέσει πνευματικῇ,**		
	through all the wisdom and understanding that the Spirit gives,		
ἐν ἐν	in/with *en*	---	prep
πάσῃ πᾶς	all *pa·sē*	DAT SG FEM	adj
σοφίᾳ σοφία	wisdom *so·phi·a*	DAT SG FEM	noun
καὶ καί	and *kai*	---	conj
συνέσει σύνεσις	understanding *syn·e·sei*	DAT SG FEM	noun
πνευματικῇ πνευματικός	spiritual *pneu·ma·ti·kē*	DAT SG FEM	adj

10a	**περιπατῆσαι ἀξίως τοῦ κυρίου**		
	so that you may live in a manner worthy of the Lord,		
περιπατῆσαι περιπατέω	to walk *pe·ri·pa·tē·sai*	AOR ACT INF	verb
ἀξίως ἀξίως	worthily *a·xi·ōs*	---	adv
τοῦ ὁ	of the *tou*	GEN SG MASC	article
κυρίου κύριος	(of) Lord *ky·ri·ou*	GEN SG MASC	noun

The manner in which a person "walks" is, for Paul, the demonstration of their participation "in Christ." If a person's truest identity is that of being "in Christ," then their life's actions, both inward and outward, will reflect that identity. This will become Paul's primary focus in the second half of the letter. See Paul's use of περιπατέω ("to walk") also in Col 2:6; 3:7; 4:5. This challenge to "walk" or live in a manner worthy of the Lord is at the heart of Paul's epistle.

10b	εἰς πᾶσαν ἀρεσκίαν		
	pleasing him in every way,		
εἰς εἰς	into/for *eis*	---	prep
πᾶσαν πᾶς	all **pa**·*san*	ACC SG FEM	adj
ἀρεσκίαν ἀρεσκεία	desire to please *a·re·**ski**·an*	ACC SG FEM	noun

10c	ἐν παντὶ ἔργῳ ἀγαθῷ καρποφοροῦντες		
	bearing fruit in every good work		
ἐν ἐν	in *en*	---	prep
παντὶ πᾶς	all/every *pan·**ti***	DAT SG NEUT	adj
ἔργῳ ἔργον	work *er·gō*	DAT SG NEUT	noun
ἀγαθῷ ἀγαθός	good *a·ga·**thō***	DAT SG NEUT	adj
καρποφοροῦντες καρποφορέω	bearing fruit *kar·po·pho·**roun**·tes*	PRES ACT PTCP NOM PL MASC	verb

This is the second time Paul has referred to "bearing fruit" since the start of the letter (see 1:6). Unlike Paul's other epistles, Colossians boasts no quotations from the Old Testament. This is one of the few times in Colossians when Paul may *allude* to a specific Old Testament text, in this case, the creation mandate of Gen 1:28: "Be fruitful, multiply and fill the earth." Here, and more clearly in 1:6, Paul uses the language of Gen 1:28 to describe the growth and spread of the gospel in the world. A similar use of Gen 1:28 can be seen in Acts 6:7; 12:24; and 19:20, where Luke describes the growth and spread of the "word of the Lord" in the world. Undoubtedly, Paul recognizes the failure of the first man and woman to "bear fruit and multiply" in the way God intended. In 1:6 he uses the language of Genesis to describe the fact that the gospel now fulfills that original call to "bear fruit and multiply." Here in v. 10, Paul adds that the goodness that was originally part of the creation of humanity and, indeed, the entirety of the creation is now extended to and through the work of the people transformed by that growing gospel. The whole world (v. 6), therefore, experiences the goodness with which it was created, now as a result of the gospel and its transformative work in the lives of God's people.

10d	καὶ αὐξανόμενοι τῇ ἐπιγνώσει τοῦ θεοῦ,		
	and growing in the knowledge of God;		
καὶ καί	and *kai*	---	conj
αὐξανόμενοι αὐξάνω	growing *au·xa·no·me·noi*	PRES PASS PTCP NOM PL MASC	verb
τῇ ὁ	to the *tē*	DAT SG FEM	article
ἐπιγνώσει ἐπίγνωσις	(to) full knowledge *e·pi·gnō·sei*	DAT SG FEM	noun
τοῦ ὁ	of the *tou*	GEN SG MASC	article
θεοῦ θεός	(of) God *the·ou*	GEN SG MASC	noun

11a	ἐν πάσῃ δυνάμει δυναμούμενοι		
	being equipped with all power		
ἐν ἐν	in/by/with *en*	---	prep
πάσῃ πᾶς	all *pa·sē*	DAT SG FEM	adj
δυνάμει δύναμις	power *dy·na·mei*	DAT SG FEM	noun
δυναμούμενοι δυναμόω	being empowered/ equipped *dy·na·mou·me·noi*	PRES PASS PTCP NOM PL MASC	verb

κατὰ τὸ κράτος τῆς δόξης αὐτοῦ

by his glorious might,

κατὰ	according to/by	---	prep
κατά	ka·ta		
τὸ	the	ACC SG NEUT	article
ὁ	to		
κράτος	strength/might	ACC SG NEUT	noun
κράτος	kra·tos		
τῆς	of the	GEN SG FEM	article
ὁ	tēs		
δόξης	(of) glory	GEN SG FEM	noun
δόξα	do·xēs		
αὐτοῦ	of him/his	GEN SG MASC	personal
αὐτός	au·tou		pron

Paul's focus in Colossians is not ultimately on Jesus' strength, but his lordship, his glory. In this case, Jesus has "glorious might" because of his lordship.

εἰς πᾶσαν ὑπομονὴν καὶ μακροθυμίαν.

so that you might have endurance and patience,

εἰς	for/into	---	prep
εἰς	eis		
πᾶσαν	all	ACC SG FEM	adj
πᾶς	pa·san		
ὑπομονὴν	perseverance/endurance	ACC SG FEM	noun
ὑπομονή	hy·po·mo·nēn		
καὶ	and	---	conj
καί	kai		
μακροθυμίαν	patience	ACC SG FEM	noun
μακροθυμία	ma·kro·thy·mi·an		

Μετὰ χαρᾶς εὐχαριστοῦντες τῷ πατρὶ τῷ ἱκανώσαντι ὑμᾶς

giving joyful thanks to the Father who has qualified you

Μετὰ	with	---	prep
μετά	Me·ta		

χαρᾶς χαρά	joy cha·**ras**	GEN SG FEM	noun
εὐχαριστοῦντες εὐχαριστέω	giving thanks eu·cha·ri·**stoun**·tes	PRES ACT PTCP NOM PL MASC	verb
τῷ ὁ	to the tō	DAT SG MASC	article
πατρὶ πατήρ	(to) father pa·**tri**	DAT SG MASC	noun
τῷ ὁ	(to) the tō	DAT SG MASC	article
ἱκανώσαντι ἱκανόω	(to) one making sufficient hi·ka·**nŏ**·san·ti	AOR ACT PTCP DAT SG MASC	verb
ὑμᾶς σύ	you (all) hy·**mas**	2ND ACC PL	personal pron

Giving thanks to God is a common refrain in Paul's letters. In Colossians, he encourages the Christians to "give thanks" to God in 1:3, 12, and 3:17.

12b   **εἰς τὴν μερίδα τοῦ κλήρου τῶν ἁγίων ἐν τῷ φωτί,**

to share in the inheritance of the saints in the kingdom of light.

εἰς εἰς	into/for eis	---	prep
τὴν ὁ	the tēn	ACC SG FEM	article
μερίδα μερίς	part/portion me·ri·da	ACC SG FEM	noun
τοῦ ὁ	of the tou	GEN SG MASC	article
κλήρου κλῆρος	(of) inheritance klē·rou	GEN SG MASC	noun
τῶν ὁ	of the tōn	GEN PL MASC	article
ἁγίων ἅγιος	(of) holy ones/saints ha·**gi**·ōn	GEN PL MASC	adj
ἐν ἐν	in en	---	prep
τῷ ὁ	the tō	DAT SG NEUT	article
φωτί φῶς	light phŏ·**ti**	DAT SG NEUT	noun

"Inheritance" (κλῆρος) is an important theme in Paul's letters, particularly as he writes to gentiles regarding their inclusion in the Abrahamic covenant (see Col 3:24; Rom 8; Gal 3:18; Eph 1:14, 18; also note Paul's emphasis on being "heirs" in Rom 4:14; 8:17). While the inheritance in the Old Testament referred in part to the land (see Deut 26:1–2; Josh 11:23), in the New Testament it refers more generally to the spiritual realities of salvation, namely, life in Christ, participation in the body of Christ, being a new creation, etc. Here, it is a participation in all the heavenly realities that come with participation in the kingdom of light, in contrast to participation in the kingdom of darkness. This dualism becomes his focus in the next verses. This dualism is also part of Paul's apocalyptic worldview, wherein there are two realities in which every aspect of creation operates: the kingdom of light (ruled over by authorities such as God, the Spirit, Jesus, Love, Peace, Goodness, etc.) and the kingdom of darkness (ruled over by authorities such as principalities, powers, Sin, Evil, Satan, Flesh, Law, etc.). What is particularly notable in this verse is that Paul brings together Israel's narratival, covenant history and the early Jewish apocalyptic worldview that only became popular in the two to three centuries before the birth of Christ. These two emphases are held together throughout Colossians (as they are in so many of Paul's epistles).

13a	ὃς ἐρύσατο ἡμᾶς ἐκ τῆς ἐξουσίας τοῦ σκότους		
	He has rescued us from the dominion of darkness		
ὃς ὅς	which *hos*	NOM SG MASC	relative pron
ἐρύσατο ῥύομαι	he delivered/rescued *e·ry·sa·to*	AOR MID IND 3RD SG	verb
ἡμᾶς ἐγώ	us *hē·mas*	1ST ACC PL	personal pron
ἐκ ἐκ	from *ek*	---	prep
τῆς ὁ	the *tēs*	GEN SG FEM	article
ἐξουσίας ἐξουσία	dominion *e·xou·si·as*	GEN SG FEM	noun
τοῦ ὁ	of the *tou*	GEN SG NEUT	article
σκότους σκότος	(of) darkness *sko·tous*	GEN SG NEUT	noun

Here again, Paul's theology is shaped by his Jewish apocalyptic world-view, in which a spiritual battle is taking place between God and evil. Christian tradition has often focused on forgiveness of sins as the primary aspect of "salvation," but salvation for Paul is more of a spiritual rescue—deliverance or liberation from enslavement to evil powers (see Rom 6). Before they participate in the life of Christ (see the discussion about participation in Christ in the "Author's Introduction"), all humans participate in and give their allegiance to the kingdom of darkness and its authorities. In fact, Paul draws on his own narratival history as a member of Israel and treats this rescue from the kingdom of darkness as a type of new exodus. In the same way that God delivered Israel from bondage to Egypt, he delivers those in Christ from a foreign power/dominion that seeks to distort the goodness of God's creation.

13b	καὶ μετέστησεν εἰς τὴν βασιλείαν τοῦ υἱοῦ τῆς ἀγάπης αὐτοῦ,		
	and transferred us into the kingdom of the Son he loves,		
καὶ καί	and *kai*	---	conj
μετέστησεν μεθίστημι	he transferred *met·e·stē·sen*	AOR ACT IND 3RD SG	verb
εἰς εἰς	into *eis*	---	prep
τὴν ὁ	the *tēn*	ACC SG FEM	article
βασιλείαν βασιλεία	kingdom *ba·si·lei·an*	ACC SG FEM	noun
τοῦ ὁ	of the *tou*	GEN SG MASC	article
υἱοῦ υἱός	(of) son *hui·ou*	GEN SG MASC	noun
τῆς ὁ	of the *tēs*	GEN SG FEM	article
ἀγάπης ἀγάπη	(of) love *a·ga·pēs*	GEN SG FEM	noun
αὐτοῦ αὐτός	of him/his *au·tou*	GEN SG MASC	personal pron

14a	ἐν ᾧ ἔχομεν τὴν ἀπολύτρωσιν,
	in whom we have redemption,

ἐν ἐν	in *en*	- - -	prep
ᾧ ὅς	whom *hō*	DAT SG MASC	relative pron
ἔχομεν ἔχω	we have *e·cho·men*	PRES ACT IND 1ST PL	verb
τὴν ὁ	the *tēn*	ACC SG FEM	article
ἀπολύτρωσιν ἀπολύτρωσις	redemption *a·po·ly·trō·sin*	ACC SG FEM	noun

God's people are redeemed *in* the Son of God. That is to say, for Paul, when a person is saved out of their slavery within the kingdom of darkness, they are brought *into* the kingdom of the Son. They are redeemed *out of* participation in evil and are redeemed *into* participation *in* the Son himself. Their identity is now found *in* the Son of God; his identity becomes their identity; what is true of him becomes true of them.

14b	τὴν ἄφεσιν τῶν ἁμαρτιῶν·
	the freedom from sins.

τὴν ὁ	the *tēn*	ACC SG FEM	article
ἄφεσιν ἄφεσις	freedom/release/forgivness *a·phe·sin*	ACC SG FEM	noun
τῶν ὁ	of the *tōn*	GEN PL FEM	article
ἁμαρτιῶν ἁμαρτία	(of) sins *ha·mar·ti·ōn*	GEN PL FEM	noun

This **ἀπολύτρωσιν** ("redemption") in v. 14a is synonymous with **ἄφεσιν** ("freedom") here in v. 14b. To be forgiven is to be delivered or liberated from the things which enslave, in this case, sins.

Big Idea. Continue to live lives worthy of the Lord.

 Bridge to Theology. In his greetings to the Colossians, Paul emphasizes that the gospel message is "bearing fruit and growing" both in Colossae and "throughout the whole world" (1:6). The believers in Colossae have accepted the gospel and are growing in their spiritual lives. One of the key themes that will be present throughout the letter is the knowledge (1:9, 10; 2:2, 3; 3:10), understanding (1:9; 2:2), and wisdom (1:28; 2:3, 23; 3:16; 4:5) of God that ought to lead believers into a life lived "worthy of the Lord" (1:10). Another key theme that Paul only hints at here is the larger apocalyptic framework behind his understanding of redemption. This theme of the kingdom or dominion of darkness vs. the kingdom of the Son emerges as the theological foundation for the entire letter. See the note about Paul's apocalyptic framework in the "Author's Introduction" at the start of this volume.

 Illustrations/Applications. If you plan to have a sermon series on Colossians, you'll undoubtedly want to take the congregation through some of the historical points: where was Colossae, who were the Colossians, what is the relationship between Paul and the Colossians, etc. The answers to these questions and more can be found in larger, traditional commentaries. Two recent and accessible commentaries that spend more than an average amount of time on these introductory matters are Gupta 2013 and McKnight 2018.

You'll also want to help your listeners begin to recognize the apocalyptic framework that dictated so much of Paul's thinking. For some congregations, the spiritual realm that is responsible for good and evil is not on their radar, and it certainly does not form the basis of their understanding of the gospel. Yet for other congregations, this might be a regular focus. In the latter case, perhaps there are aspects of Paul's early Jewish apocalyptic framework that can be expanded or developed (e.g., the two kingdoms that define all of reality). If you want your listeners to hear Paul's message in Colossians, they must first begin to understand the first-century Jewish worldview that informed Paul's understanding of who Jesus was and what he was truly about.

This would also be a golden opportunity to share with the congregation how much of a gift it is to be able to serve them, teach them, pray for them, and watch them grow in the wisdom and knowledge that the Spirit gives. One of the most blessed callings (even though at times it certainly may not feel this way) is the calling to shepherd God's flock. Share with your people how much you cherish them and what a joy it is to serve them.

CHRIST'S SUPREMACY AND THE COLOSSIANS' REDEMPTION

Perhaps the most beautiful depiction of Paul's gospel is here in these verses: Jesus Christ is Lord of creation, and through his death within that creation, he reconciled every created thing to God, including us, the very enemies of God.

15a ὅς ἐστιν εἰκὼν τοῦ θεοῦ τοῦ ἀοράτου,

hos estin eikōn tou theou tou aoratou,

He is the image of the invisible God,

15b πρωτότοκος πάσης κτίσεως,

prōtotokos pasēs ktiseōs,

the firstborn of all creation,

16a ὅτι ἐν αὐτῷ ἐκτίσθη τὰ πάντα

hoti en autō ektisthē ta panta

since in him all things were created,

16b ἐν τοῖς οὐρανοῖς καὶ ἐπὶ τῆς γῆς,

en tois ouranois kai epi tēs gēs,

things in heaven and on earth,

16c τὰ ὁρατὰ καὶ τὰ ἀόρατα,

ta horata kai ta aorata,

visible and invisible,

16d εἴτε θρόνοι εἴτε κυριότητες

eite thronoi eite kyriotētes

whether thrones or dominions

16e εἴτε ἀρχαὶ εἴτε ἐξουσίαι·

eite archai eite exousiai;

or rulers or authorities.

16f τὰ πάντα δι᾽ αὐτοῦ καὶ εἰς αὐτὸν ἔκτισται·

ta panta di᾽ autou kai eis auton ektistai;

All things have been created through him and for him.

καὶ αὐτός ἔστιν πρὸ πάντων

kai autos estin pro pantōn

And he is before all things,

17b

καὶ τὰ πάντα ἐν αὐτῷ συνέστηκεν,

kai ta panta en autō synestēken,

and in him all things hold together.

15a	ὅς ἐστιν εἰκὼν τοῦ θεοῦ τοῦ ἀοράτου,		
	He is the image of the invisible God,		
ὅς ὅς	who *hos*	NOM SG MASC	relative pron
ἐστιν εἰμί	(he) is *e·stin*	PRES ACT IND 3RD SG	verb
εἰκὼν εἰκών	image *ei·kōn*	NOM SG FEM	noun
τοῦ ὁ	of the *tou*	GEN SG MASC	article
θεοῦ θεός	(of) God *the·ou*	GEN SG MASC	noun
τοῦ ὁ	(of) the *tou*	GEN SG MASC	article
ἀοράτου ἀόρατος	(of) invisible *a·o·ra·tou*	GEN SG MASC	adj

This verse begins with a relative pronoun, connecting it back to the iden-
tification of the Son in 1:13–14. That Jesus is the "image of the invisible
God" here is similar to the description of Jesus as the "form of God" in
Phil 2:6. Jesus is the incarnate God (John 1:14). He reveals the invisible
God in his humanity.

15b	**πρωτότοκος πάσης κτίσεως,**
	the firstborn of all creation,

πρωτότοκος	firstborn	NOM SG MASC	adj
πρωτότοκος	prō·to·to·kos		
πάσης	of all	GEN SG FEM	adj
πᾶς	pa·sēs		
κτίσεως	(of) creation	GEN SG FEM	noun
κτίσις	kti·se·ōs		

The implication here is not that Jesus was created, like every other human, but rather that he has the supremacy over all creation. "Firstborn" (**πρωτότοκος**) in Jewish culture referred not merely to the order of birth but to the responsibilities, privileges, and powers that came with being born first. Jesus has authority and power over all creation. We're told in 1:13 that Jesus is the beloved Son of God; here we're told that he is the beloved *firstborn* Son, emphasizing both his primacy over creation and his familial rank as the Son of God.

16a	**ὅτι ἐν αὐτῷ ἐκτίσθη τὰ πάντα**
	since in him all things were created,

ὅτι	since/because	---	conj
ὅτι	ho·ti		
ἐν	in/by/through	---	prep
ἐν	en		
αὐτῷ	him	DAT SG MASC	personal
αὐτός	au·tō		pron
ἐκτίσθη	they were [lit., (it) was] created	AOR PASS IND 3RD SG	verb
κτίζω	e·ktis·thē		
τὰ	the (things)	NOM PL NEUT	article
ὁ	ta		
πάντα	all (things)	NOM PL NEUT	adj
πᾶς	pan·ta		

Here we must choose between the use of "in" or "by" as the best translations for ἐν. Given Paul's emphasis on "in Christ" throughout the letter, it is best to translate this use of the preposition in this way also. It is not just that all things were created *by means of* or *through* Christ, but rather it is the identity, power, supremacy of Christ *as God himself* that enabled him to be able to be the means by which all things are created. The emphasis is not placed on what Christ does but on what Christ does *as* the image of God. In him resides the ability to create all things.

16b	ἐν τοῖς οὐρανοῖς καὶ ἐπὶ τῆς γῆς,		
	things in heaven and on earth,		
ἐν ἐν	in/by *en*	---	prep
τοῖς ὁ	the *tois*	DAT PL MASC	article
οὐρανοῖς οὐρανός	heavens *ou·ra·nois*	DAT PL MASC	noun
καὶ καί	and *kai*	---	conj
ἐπὶ ἐπί	on/over *e·pi*	---	prep
τῆς ὁ	the *tēs*	GEN SG FEM	article
γῆς γῆ	earth *gēs*	GEN SG FEM	noun

16c	τὰ ὁρατὰ καὶ τὰ ἀόρατα,		
	visible and invisible,		
τὰ ὁ	the (things) *ta*	NOM PL NEUT	article
ὁρατὰ ὁρατός	visible (things) *ho·ra·ta*	NOM PL NEUT	adj
καὶ καί	and *kai*	---	conj
τὰ ὁ	the (things) *ta*	NOM PL NEUT	article
ἀόρατα ἀόρατος	invisible (things) *a·o·ra·ta*	NOM PL NEUT	adj

Things "in heaven and on earth, visible and invisible" refer to the same realities: the spiritual, unseen realm of heaven and the physical, visible realm of earth. This is likely a reference back to Gen 1:1: "In the beginning, God created the heavens and the earth." We now know that God created all things *in* and *through* Christ, the beloved firstborn Son who reigns over the kingdom of God.

εἴτε θρόνοι εἴτε κυριότητες			
whether thrones or dominions			
εἴτε εἴτε	whether *ei·te*	---	conj
θρόνοι θρόνος	thrones ***thro***·*noi*	NOM PL MASC	noun
εἴτε εἴτε	whether *ei·te*	---	conj
κυριότητες κυριότης	authorities/lordships/ dominions *ky·ri·**o**·tēs*	NOM PL FEM	noun

εἴτε ἀρχαὶ εἴτε ἐξουσίαι·			
or rulers or authorities.			
εἴτε εἴτε	whether *ei·te*	---	conj
ἀρχαὶ ἀρχή	rulers *ar·**chai***	NOM PL FEM	noun
εἴτε εἴτε	whether *ei·te*	---	conj
ἐξουσίαι ἐξουσία	authorities *e·xou·**si**·ai*	NOM PL FEM	noun

Thrones, dominions, rulers, and authorities encapsulate every power in existence that is in competition with the power and authority of Christ. These are the powers that rule in the dominion of darkness, the realm of existence in which we formerly existed and out of which we have been rescued (1:14; see also Rom 8:38; 1 Cor 8:5; Eph 1:21; 6:12).

τὰ πάντα δι᾽ αὐτοῦ καὶ εἰς αὐτὸν ἔκτισται·			
All things have been created through him and for him.			
τὰ ὁ	the (things) *ta*	NOM PL NEUT	article
πάντα πᾶς	all (things) ***pan***·*ta*	NOM PL NEUT	adj
δι᾽ διά	through/because of *di᾽*	---	prep

αὐτοῦ	him	GEN SG MASC	personal
αὐτός	*au·tou*		pron
καὶ	and	---	conj
καί	*kai*		
εἰς	for	---	prep
εἰς	*eis*		
αὐτὸν	him	ACC SG MASC	personal
αὐτός	*au·ton*		pron
ἔκτισται	(it) has been created	PERF PASS IND	verb
κτίζω	*e·kti·stai*	3RD SG	

At the beginning of this verse, the emphasis is on the arena in which all things were created: "in" Christ. Now at the end of the verse, two additional prepositions are used to communicate the relationship between Christ and the creation of all things: **δι'** ("through") and **εἰς** ("for"). That is to say that Christ is the source, the instrument, and the goal of creation.

17a	καὶ αὐτός ἔστιν πρὸ πάντων		
	And he is before all things,		
καὶ	and	---	conj
καί	*kai*		
αὐτὸς	he	NOM SG MASC	personal
αὐτός	*au·tos*		pron
ἔστιν	(he) is	PRES ACT IND	verb
εἰμί	*e·stin*	3RD SG	
πρὸ	before	---	prep
πρό	*pro*		
πάντων	all (things)	GEN PL MASC	adj
πᾶς	*pan·tōn*		

Another key preposition is used to describe Christ's temporal superiority to creation: **πρὸ** ("before").

17b	καὶ τὰ πάντα ἐν αὐτῷ συνέστηκεν,		
	and in him all things hold together.		
καὶ	and	---	conj
καί	*kai*		
τὰ	the	NOM PL NEUT	article
ὁ	*ta*		

πάντα πᾶς	all (things) **pan**·ta	NOM PL NEUT	adj
ἐν ἐν	in/by/with en	---	prep
αὐτῷ αὐτός	him au·**tō**	DAT SG MASC	personal pron
συνέστηκεν συνίστημι	(it) has stood together syn·e·stē·ken	PERF ACT IND 3RD SG	verb

See also Heb 1:3.

18a
καὶ αὐτός ἐστιν ἡ κεφαλὴ τοῦ σώματος,

kai autos estin hē kephalē tou sōmatos,

He is the head of the body,

18b
τῆς ἐκκλησίας·

tēs ekklēsias;

the church;

18c
ὅς ἐστιν ἀρχή,

hos estin archē,

he is the beginning,

18d
πρωτότοκος ἐκ τῶν νεκρῶν,

prōtotokos ek tōn nekrōn,

the firstborn from the dead,

18e
ἵνα γένηται ἐν πᾶσιν αὐτὸς πρωτεύων,

hina genētai en pasin autos prōteuōn,

in order that he might become supreme in all things.

19
ὅτι ἐν αὐτῷ εὐδόκησεν πᾶν τὸ πλήρωμα κατοικῆσαι

hoti en autō eudokēsen pan to plērōma katoikēsai

For God in all his fullness was pleased to dwell in him

20a
καὶ δι᾽ αὐτοῦ ἀποκαταλλάξαι τὰ πάντα εἰς αὐτόν,

kai di' autou apokatallaxai ta panta eis auton,

and through him to reconcile all things to himself,

20b
εἰρηνοποιήσας διὰ τοῦ αἵματος τοῦ σταυροῦ αὐτοῦ,

eirēnopoiēsas dia tou haimatos tou staurou autou,

making peace through the blood of his cross,

20c
[δι᾽ αὐτοῦ]

[di' autou]

through him,

20d

εἴτε τὰ ἐπὶ τῆς γῆς

eite ta epi tēs gēs

whether things on earth

20e

εἴτε τὰ ἐν τοῖς οὐρανοῖς·

eite ta en tois ouranois;

or things in heaven.

<table>
<tr><td colspan="4">18a   καὶ αὐτός ἐστιν ἡ κεφαλὴ τοῦ σώματος,</td></tr>
<tr><td colspan="4">He is the head of the body,</td></tr>
</table>

καὶ	and	---	conj
καί	*kai*		
αὐτός	he	NOM SG MASC	personal
αὐτός	*au·tos*		pron
ἐστιν	(he) is	PRES ACT IND	verb
εἰμί	*e·stin*	3RD SG	
ἡ	the	NOM SG FEM	article
ὁ	*hē*		
κεφαλὴ	head	NOM SG FEM	noun
κεφαλή	*ke·pha·lē*		
τοῦ	of the	GEN SG NEUT	article
ὁ	*tou*		
σώματος	(of) body	GEN SG NEUT	noun
σῶμα	*sō·ma·tos*		

<table>
<tr><td colspan="4">18b   τῆς ἐκκλησίας·</td></tr>
<tr><td colspan="4">the church;</td></tr>
</table>

τῆς	of the	GEN SG FEM	article
ὁ	*tēs*		
ἐκκλησίας	(of) church	GEN SG FEM	noun
ἐκκλησία	*ek·klē·si·as*		

That Christ is the "head" (**κεφαλὴ**) of the body, the church, here is a reminder that the Colossian Christians are united together and have their being in one location: Christ himself. For Paul, this language is not an empty metaphor. The church is united *in* Christ; the church therefore represents Christ on earth. And, just as the rest of creation is established and sustained in and through and for Christ, so also is the church.

18c	**ὅς ἐστιν ἀρχή,**			
	he is the beginning,			
ὅς ὅς	which *hos*	NOM SG MASC	relative pron
ἐστιν εἰμί	(he) is *e·stin*	PRES ACT IND 3RD SG	verb
ἀρχή ἀρχή	beginning/ruler *ar·chē*	NOM SG FEM	noun

The use of **ἀρχή** here is intriguing, considering it means "beginning" and "ruler." In this case, "beginning" is likely to be the emphasis, particularly given the following clause, but the direction of the verse is toward the recognition that Christ is "supreme in all things." That is to say, the beginning of the new creation is launched in Christ's resurrection from the dead. Additionally, his defeat of death in his resurrection indicates that he is, in fact, ruler of all things. He is in every way the true **ἀρχή**, the true "beginning" and the true "ruler."

18d	**πρωτότοκος ἐκ τῶν νεκρῶν,**			
	the firstborn from the dead,			
πρωτότοκος πρωτότοκος	firstborn *prō·to·to·kos*	NOM SG MASC	adj
ἐκ ἐκ	from *ek*	---	prep
τῶν ὁ	the *tōn*	GEN PL MASC	article
νεκρῶν νεκρός	dead (ones) *ne·krōn*	GEN PL MASC	adj

ἵνα γένηται ἐν πᾶσιν αὐτὸς πρωτεύων,

in order that he might become supreme in all things.

ἵνα	in order that/that	---	conj
ἵνα	*hi·na*		
γένηται	he might become	AOR MID SUBJ	verb
γίνομαι	*ge·nē·tai*	3RD SG	
ἐν	in	---	prep
ἐν	*en*		
πᾶσιν	all (things)	DAT PL NEUT	adj
πᾶς	*pa·sin*		
αὐτὸς	he	NOM SG MASC	personal
αὐτός	*au·tos*		pron
πρωτεύων	(he) is preeminent/supreme	PRES ACT PTCP	verb
πρωτεύω	*prō·teu·ōn*	NOM SG MASC	

Whereas in 1:15 Christ was the "firstborn" over all creation, he is now the "firstborn" from the dead. That is, he is the first to exist within the new creation and therefore has supremacy over the new creation, which includes the Colossian Christians themselves.

19 ὅτι ἐν αὐτῷ εὐδόκησεν πᾶν τὸ πλήρωμα κατοικῆσαι

For God in all his fullness was pleased to dwell in him

ὅτι	that/since/because	---	conj
ὅτι	*ho·ti*		
ἐν	in	---	prep
ἐν	*en*		
αὐτῷ	him	DAT SG MASC	personal
αὐτός	*au·tō*		pron
εὐδόκησεν	he was well pleased	AOR ACT IND	verb
εὐδοκέω	*eu·do·kē·sen*	3RD SG	
πᾶν	all	NOM SG NEUT	adj
πᾶς	*pan*		
τὸ	the	NOM SG NEUT	article
ὁ	*to*		
πλήρωμα	fullness	NOM SG NEUT	noun
πλήρωμα	*plē·rō·ma*		
κατοικῆσαι	to dwell	AOR ACT INF	verb
κατοικέω	*kat·oi·kē·sai*		

The subject of the clause is **πᾶν τὸ πλήρωμα** ("all the fullness"). Here Paul employs this to refer to the "fullness of God," so that ultimately "God in all his fullness" becomes the subject of the clause.

20a	**καὶ δι᾽ αὐτοῦ ἀποκαταλλάξαι τὰ πάντα εἰς αὐτόν,**		
	and through him to reconcile all things to himself,		
καὶ καί	and *kai*	---	conj
δι᾽ διά	through/because of *di᾽*	---	prep
αὐτοῦ αὐτός	him *au·tou*	GEN SG MASC	personal pron
ἀποκαταλλάξαι ἀποκαταλλάσσω	to reconcile *a·po·ka·tal·la·xai*	AOR ACT INF	verb
τὰ ὁ	the (things) *ta*	ACC PL NEUT	article
πάντα πᾶς	all (things) *pan·ta*	ACC PL NEUT	adj
εἰς εἰς	into/for *eis*	---	prep
αὐτόν αὐτός	him *au·ton*	ACC SG MASC	personal pron

The language of reconciliation in this verse is reminiscent of the language found in 2 Cor 5:19 and Rom 5:10. However, while in these other Pauline texts the word for reconciliation is **καταλλάσσω** ("to reconcile"), the word used for reconciliation here (**ἀποκαταλλάσσω**) is slightly different and is found only here in 1:20, 22 and in Eph 2:16). The inclusion of the prefix **ἀπο-** ("back") at the start of the word might imply a turning back to God or indicate finality or completeness. It may even imply both: that God has reconciled all things in creation back to himself, to be completely his as originally intended. We can think of a scenario where a child has a toy stolen from her by another child. When she takes it back, she is reconciled with what was hers originally. This may be the case here, especially given the theme of competing kingdoms and rulers within Colossians.

It is difficult to know exactly what Paul intended, but Christ is likely the antecedent of **δι᾽ αὐτοῦ** ("through him"), while God is the antecedent of **εἰς αὐτόν** ("to him/himself"). We are reconciled to God through Christ. But "we" does not refer to humans alone. All of creation is reconciled to God through Christ. Paul's gospel is a cosmic gospel, one which proclaims "good news" for the entirety of the disrupted cosmos. Paul makes it clear in Rom 8:18–22 that the entirety of the created order was disrupted by humanity's rejection of their divine image-bearing responsibilities. Here Paul makes it clear that Christ's work of redemption means reconciliation for *all things.*

20b	εἰρηνοποιήσας διὰ τοῦ αἵματος τοῦ σταυροῦ αὐτοῦ,		
	making peace through the blood of his cross,		
εἰρηνοποιήσας εἰρηνοποιέω	making peace *ei·rē·no·poi·ē·sas*	AOR ACT PTCP NOM SG MASC	verb
διὰ διά	through/because of *di·a*		prep
τοῦ ὁ	the *tou*	GEN SG NEUT	article
αἵματος αἷμα	blood *hai·ma·tos*	GEN SG NEUT	noun
τοῦ ὁ	of the *tou*	GEN SG MASC	article
σταυροῦ σταυρός	(of) cross *stau·rou*	GEN SG MASC	noun
αὐτοῦ αὐτός	of him/his *au·tou*	GEN SG MASC	personal pron

Here, as in 1:2, "peace" does not refer to some form of inner tranquility, as it is often described today. The use here points forward to the use in 3:15, where this "peace making" is the goal of redemption. It is a redemption wherein creational disruption or relational discord is eradicated and the anticipated flourishing of Gen 1–2 is actualized. As we'll see in a few verses, it is a peace that comes as a result of the defeat of evil. The spiritual battle that led to the defeat of evil happened not in the resurrection, as it is often portrayed in some Christian Easter services, but through Christ's death. Good Friday is in some ways more theologically significant in Pauline theology than Easter Sunday.

20c	[δι' αὐτοῦ]		
	through him,		
δι' διά	through/because of *di'*	---	prep
αὐτοῦ αὐτός	him/it *au·tou*	GEN SG MASC	personal pron

This additional **δι' αὐτοῦ** ("through him") is grammatically unnecessary. Its addition acts in the same way as our italics; it makes obvious where the emphasis lies—in this case, on the person of Jesus Christ.

20d	**εἴτε τὰ ἐπὶ τῆς γῆς**		
	whether things on earth		
εἴτε εἴτε	whether *ei·te*	---	conj
τὰ ὁ	the (things) *ta*	ACC PL NEUT	article
ἐπὶ ἐπί	upon/on *e·pi*	---	prep
τῆς ὁ	the *tēs*	GEN SG FEM	article
γῆς γῆ	earth *gēs*	GEN SG FEM	noun

20e	**εἴτε τὰ ἐν τοῖς οὐρανοῖς·**		
	or things in heaven.		
εἴτε εἴτε	whether *ei·te*	---	conj
τὰ ὁ	the (things) *ta*	ACC PL NEUT	article
ἐν ἐν	in *en*	---	prep
τοῖς ὁ	the *tois*	DAT PL MASC	article
οὐρανοῖς οὐρανός	heavens *ou·ra·nois*	DAT PL MASC	noun

"Things on earth" and "things in heaven" literally encapsulate everything in existence. Christ is Lord in every sphere of existence, and so redemption is possible within every sphere of existence.

21a

καὶ ὑμᾶς ποτὲ ὄντας ἀπηλλοτριωμένους

kai hymas pote ontas apēllotriōmenous

καὶ ἐχθροὺς τῇ διανοίᾳ

kai echthrous tē dianoia

**And you were once alienated from God
and were enemies in your minds,**

21b

ἐν τοῖς ἔργοις τοῖς πονηροῖς,

en tois ergois tois ponērois,

doing evil deeds.

22a

—νυνὶ δὲ ἀποκατήλλαξεν ἐν τῷ σώματι τῆς σαρκὸς αὐτοῦ

—nyni de apokatēllaxen en tō sōmati tēs sarkos autou

But now, he has reconciled you in his physical body

22b

διὰ τοῦ θανάτου,

dia tou thanatou,

through death

22c

—παραστῆσαι ὑμᾶς ἁγίους καὶ ἀμώμους

—parastēsai hymas hagious kai amōmous

καὶ ἀνεγκλήτους κατενώπιον αὐτοῦ,

kai anenklētous katenōpion autou,

**to present you holy and unblemished
and blameless in his presence,**

23a

εἴ γε ἐπιμένετε τῇ πίστει

ei ge epimenete tē pistei

if you persevere in the faith (and I know you will),

23b

τεθεμελιωμένοι καὶ ἑδραῖοι

tethemeliōmenoi kai hedraioi

having been established and firm,

23c καὶ μὴ μετακινούμενοι ἀπὸ τῆς ἐλπίδος

kai mē metakinoumenoi apo tēs elpidos

τοῦ εὐαγγελίου οὗ ἠκούσατε,

tou euangeliou hou ēkousate,

not moving from the hope of the gospel which you heard,

23d τοῦ κηρυχθέντος ἐν πάσῃ κτίσει τῇ ὑπὸ τὸν οὐρανόν,

tou kērychthentos en pasē ktisei tē hypo ton ouranon,

which has been proclaimed in all creation under heaven,

23e οὗ ἐγενόμην ἐγὼ Παῦλος διάκονος.

hou egenomēn egō Paulos diakonos.

and of which I, Paul, became a minister.

21a	**καὶ ὑμᾶς ποτὲ ὄντας ἀπηλλοτριωμένους καὶ ἐχθροὺς τῇ διανοίᾳ**		
	And you were once alienated from God and were enemies in your minds,		
καὶ καί	and *kai*	---	conj
ὑμᾶς σύ	you *hy·mas*	2ND ACC PL	personal pron
ποτὲ ποτέ	formerly/once/when *po·te*	---	particle
ὄντας εἰμί	(those) being *on·tas*	PRES ACT PTCP ACC PL MASC	verb
ἀπηλλοτριωμένους ἀπαλλοτριόω	(those) having been alienated *a·pēl·lo·tri·ō·me·nous*	PERF PASS PTCP ACC PL MASC	verb
καὶ καί	and *kai*	---	conj
ἐχθροὺς ἐχθρός	hostile/enemy-like (ones) *ech·throus*	ACC PL MASC	adj
τῇ ὁ	in/to/with the *tē*	DAT SG FEM	article

| διανοίᾳ | thought/mind | DAT SG FEM | noun |
| διάνοια | di·a·**noi**·a | | |

The high christological declaration in 1:15–20 is a side note, a theological rationale for why Paul can say what he does in 1:11–14 and 1:21–22. After the declaration of the Lordship of Christ in vv. 15–20, Paul now returns to the point he began to make at the end of 1:12, reiterating that the Colossian Christians were once participants in the kingdom of darkness (1:13). Paul uses ἐχθρός here which can be rendered "hostile" or "enemies." In this case, if "hostile" is chosen, it covers up the spiritual battle that Paul understood to be taking place. Using the word "enemies," on the other hand, communicates that there are two sides in the spiritual battle—the kingdom of light and the kingdom of darkness—and Paul understood the Colossians to be active soldiers within the kingdom of darkness. It is not just that the Colossians rejected God in their hearts or were left out of the equation altogether. They were armed enemies of God, fighting for the other side.

21b	ἐν τοῖς ἔργοις τοῖς πονηροῖς,		
	doing evil deeds.		
ἐν	in/by/with	---	prep
ἐν	en		
τοῖς	the	DAT PL NEUT	article
ὁ	tois		
ἔργοις	works	DAT PL NEUT	noun
ἔργον	er·gois		
τοῖς	the	DAT PL NEUT	article
ὁ	tois		
πονηροῖς	evil (ones)	DAT PL NEUT	adj
πονηρός	po·nē·**rois**		

Paul indicates by these words that it was through evil deeds that the Colossians alienated themselves from God. By choosing to actively participate in evil, they also were choosing to act as enemies of God.

22a	—νυνὶ δὲ ἀποκατήλλαξεν ἐν τῷ σώματι τῆς σαρκὸς αὐτοῦ		
	But now, he has reconciled you in his physical body		
νυνὶ	now	---	adv
νυνί	ny·**ni**		

δὲ δέ	but *de*	---	conj
ἀποκατήλλαξεν ἀποκαταλλάσσω	he reconciled *a·po·kat·ēl·la·xen*	AOR ACT IND 3RD SG	verb
ἐν ἐν	in/by/with *en*	---	prep
τῷ ὁ	the *tō*	DAT SG NEUT	article
σώματι σῶμα	body *sō·ma·ti*	DAT SG NEUT	noun
τῆς ὁ	of the *tēs*	GEN SG FEM	article
σαρκὸς σάρξ	(of) flesh *sar·kos*	GEN SG FEM	noun
αὐτοῦ αὐτός	of him/his *au·tou*	GEN SG MASC	personal pron

Paul begins this line with **νυνὶ δὲ** ("but now"), emphasizing the fundamental shift in their identity: they were *formerly* enemies of God (1:21), needing to be rescued from the kingdom of darkness (1:13), *but now* they are reconciled to God (1:22), redeemed by God (1:14), having been brought into the kingdom of light/Son (1:12, 13). *Therefore,* they ought to live lives worthy of the Lord (1:10) in all that that implies. They no longer exist in the realm of evil but in the realm of God. So, they ought to live like it.

This is one of the few times that Paul uses **σάρξ** ("flesh") as a neutral reference to a physical body rather than to an evil power at work (i.e., "Flesh") See also 1:24.

Note also that, while Paul does not explicitly say "you" in this verse, he is clearly directing his comments to the Colossian believers, who now find themselves reconciled to God.

22b	**διὰ τοῦ θανάτου,**		
	through death,		
διὰ διά	through/because of *di·a*	---	prep
τοῦ ὁ	the *tou*	GEN SG MASC	article
θανάτου θάνατος	death *tha·na·tou*	GEN SG MASC	noun

—παραστῆσαι ὑμᾶς ἁγίους καὶ ἀμώμους καὶ ἀνεγκλήτους κατενώπιον αὐτοῦ,

to present you holy and unblemished
and blameless in his presence,

παραστῆσαι παρίστημι	to be present/stand alongside pa·ra·**stē**·sai	AOR ACT INF	verb
ὑμᾶς σύ	you (all) hy·**mas**	2ND ACC PL	personal pron
ἁγίους ἅγιος	holy (ones)/saints ha·**gi**·ous	ACC PL MASC	adj
καὶ καί	and **kai**	---	conj
ἀμώμους ἄμωμος	unblemished/faultless (ones) a·**mō**·mous	ACC PL MASC	adj
καὶ καί	and **kai**	---	conj
ἀνεγκλήτους ἀνέγκλητος	blameless (ones) an·en·**klē**·tous	ACC PL MASC	adj
κατενώπιον κατενώπιον	before/in the presence of kat·e·**nō**·pi·on	---	prep
αὐτοῦ αὐτός	him au·**tou**	GEN SG MASC	personal pron

Undertones of the Jewish sacrificial system are woven throughout these words. It is particularly evident in the use of **ἄμωμος** ("unblemished") as a description of the sacrifice the priest would present to God (e.g., Lev 4:3, 23).

εἴ γε ἐπιμένετε τῇ πίστει

if you persevere in the faith (and I know you will),

εἴ εἰ	if *ei*	---	cond
γε γέ	indeed *ge*	---	particle
ἐπιμένετε ἐπιμένω	you remain/continue e·pi·**me**·ne·te	PRES ACT IND 2ND PL	verb
τῇ ὁ	in (the) *tē*	DAT SG FEM	article
πίστει πίστις	faith **pi**·stei	DAT SG FEM	noun

Though this is written as a conditional clause—"if [εἰ] you continue"—Paul is confident that they will continue or, more likely, persevere, hence his use of a present active indicative verb. Paul also uses here the definite article with "faith," τῇ πίστει, likely referring to the gospel message that Paul preached and which they had previously accepted (which Paul returns to at the end of this verse).

23b	τεθεμελιωμένοι καὶ ἑδραῖοι		
	having been established and firm,		
τεθεμελιωμένοι	having been established/ founded	PERF PASS PTCP NOM PL MASC	verb
θεμελιόω	te·the·me·li·ō·**me**·noi		
καὶ	and	---	conj
καί	**kai**		
ἑδραῖοι	firm/steadfast	NOM PL MASC	adj
ἑδραῖος	he·**drai**·oi		

23c	καὶ μὴ μετακινούμενοι ἀπὸ τῆς ἐλπίδος τοῦ εὐαγγελίου οὗ ἠκούσατε,		
	not moving from the hope of the gospel which you heard,		
καὶ	and	---	conj
καί	**kai**		
μὴ	not	---	particle
μή	**mē**		
μετακινούμενοι	being moved away/ shifting	PRES PASS PTCP NOM PL MASC	verb
μετακινέω	me·ta·ki·**nou**·me·noi		
ἀπὸ	from	---	prep
ἀπό	a·**po**		
τῆς	the	GEN SG FEM	article
ὁ	**tēs**		
ἐλπίδος	hope	GEN SG FEM	noun
ἐλπίς	el·**pi**·dos		
τοῦ	of the	GEN SG NEUT	article
ὁ	**tou**		
εὐαγγελίου	(of) gospel	GEN SG NEUT	noun
εὐαγγέλιον	eu·an·ge·**li**·ou		
οὗ	of which	GEN SG NEUT	relative pron
ὅς	**hou**		
ἠκούσατε	you heard	AOR ACT IND 2ND PL	verb
ἀκούω	ē·**kou**·sa·te		

τοῦ κηρυχθέντος ἐν πάσῃ κτίσει τῇ ὑπὸ τὸν οὐρανόν,

which has been proclaimed in all creation under heaven,

Greek	English	Parsing	Part
τοῦ ὁ	of the *tou*	GEN SG NEUT	article
κηρυχθέντος κηρύσσω	of (it) being proclaimed/ preached *kē·rych·then·tos*	AOR PASS PTCP GEN SG NEUT	verb
ἐν ἐν	in/by/with *en*	---	prep
πάσῃ πᾶς	all/every *pa·sē*	DAT SG FEM	adj
κτίσει κτίσις	creature/creation *kti·sei*	DAT SG FEM	noun
τῇ ὁ	(the) *tē*	DAT SG FEM	article
ὑπὸ ὑπό	under *hy·po*	---	prep
τὸν ὁ	(the) *ton*	ACC SG MASC	article
οὐρανόν οὐρανός	heaven *ou·ra·non*	ACC SG MASC	noun

The reader will notice that the article **τῇ** is not translated. In this case, it indicates that the prepositional phrase that follows is to be read as a relative clause modifying **κτίσει** (with which **τῇ** agrees): "all creation (which is) under heaven."

οὗ ἐγενόμην ἐγὼ Παῦλος διάκονος.

and of which I, Paul, became a minister.

Greek	English	Parsing	Part
οὗ ὅς	of which *hou*	GEN SG NEUT	relative pron
ἐγενόμην γίνομαι	(I) became *e·ge·no·mēn*	AOR MID IND 1ST SG	verb
ἐγὼ ἐγώ	I *e·gō*	1ST NOM SG	personal pron
Παῦλος Παῦλος	Paul *Pau·los*	NOM SG MASC	noun
διάκονος διάκονος	minister/servant *di·a·ko·nos*	NOM SG MASC	noun

Paul concludes this section with hyperbole (the gospel message has surely *not* been proclaimed in *all* of creation). In doing so, he reminds the Colossian Christians again about the cosmic significance of the gospel message and the way in which they have all been caught up in it, himself included.

Big Idea. The Lord of creation has reconciled all of creation to God, including us, the enemies of God.

 Bridge to Theology. This is perhaps one of the most theologically loaded passages of the entire New Testament. There are four key theological points to be made here. (1) This passage is first and foremost about the identity of Jesus as the divine God, Yahweh, who created all things in Gen 1:1–31. It is easy, but misguided, to think about "God" as the God of the Old Testament and then Jesus somehow adding to the identity of God in the New Testament. Jesus is the same God of the Old Testament. He was not only there at creation but "in him" and "by him" all things were created (1:16). This is the identity that grants him the title "Lord." (2) As Lord, Jesus is also the head of the church, the firstborn of the dead (1:18). This means that in his humanity, he is head of the new creation, the new Adam, the representative of a new humanity. (3) Redemption is about both reconciliation and forgiveness. We were once enemies of God, fighting actively against God in his good creation. In his grace, he has transferred us from the kingdom of darkness (1:13) and into his own kingdom, over which he rules as Lord (1:13). He declares us holy and free from accusation (1:22), not as those who no longer sin, but as those who are no longer his enemies. (4) Redemption is for the entire cosmos. All things in creation *are reconciled* to God in Jesus Christ (1:20). If there are verses in the Pauline epistles that ought to make us stop and question what we believe, this is one of them.

 Illustrations/Applications. Part of what Paul means by "all the wisdom and understanding that the Spirit gives" in 1:9 is an understanding (as much as we are able) of who Jesus is. Sometimes just learning theology or being reminded of incredible truths regarding our faith and our God is enough "application" in itself. Learning about God is worship. If your congregation needs a reminder of these theological truths, then perhaps that approach is more important than finding three points of "practical" application.

If your congregation needs a reminder that the gospel is intended to touch and transform the world beyond the spiritual life of the individual, here would be an excellent opportunity to emphasize this gospel truth. In what ways does the version of the gospel we present impact the environment (i.e., all creation)? Or our political systems? Or our economic systems? How ought the gospel transform even our own personal budgets? Or how we view other denominations with very different theological viewpoints than our own? Perhaps there are ways that we can begin asking and answering these questions on the basis of this cosmic gospel.

For Paul, the ultimate goal of the cross was the establishment of peace (1:20), which is one more way of saying that the gospel is about more than just forgiveness of the individual. This "peace" is a peace that reflects the shalom of the garden of Eden, when the created order was characterized by love, harmony, unity, and goodness. Where do we strive for gospel peace? What systems or arenas in our society, church, or lives need this cosmic peace? How about our relationships with one another, or with other churches in our cities? The troubling part of these questions is just how easy it is to find areas of our world today that need this cross-bestowed peace.

"Make me an instrument of your peace."

THE MYSTERY OF CHRIST AND THE MINISTRY OF SERVICE

We see in these verses the true calling of a pastor: suffering, struggling, and contending on behalf of those to whom she or he is called to proclaim the gospel of Christ, including on behalf of those who may never know the pastor in person. Paul's ministry is a ministry of true self-sacrifice and service.

24a   Νῦν χαίρω ἐν τοῖς παθήμασιν ὑπὲρ ὑμῶν,

*Nyn chairō en **tois** pathēmasin **hyper** hymōn,*

Now I rejoice in my sufferings on your behalf,

24b   καὶ ἀνταναπληρῶ τὰ ὑστερήματα τῶν θλίψεων τοῦ χριστοῦ

*kai antanaplērō **ta** hysterēmata **tōn thlipseōn tou** christou*

and I fill up in turn what is lacking in the afflictions of Christ

24c   ἐν τῇ σαρκί μου

*en **tē** sarki mou*

in my flesh,

24d   ὑπὲρ τοῦ σώματος αὐτοῦ,

*hyper **tou** sōmatos **autou**,*

for the sake of his body,

24e   ὅ ἐστιν ἡ ἐκκλησία,

***ho** estin hē ekklēsia,*

the church.

25a   ἧς ἐγενόμην ἐγὼ διάκονος

hēs egenomēn egō diakonos

I became its servant

25b   κατὰ τὴν οἰκονομίαν τοῦ θεοῦ

*kata **tēn** oikonomian **tou** theou*

by God's commission

25c   τὴν δοθεῖσάν μοι εἰς ὑμᾶς

*tēn dotheisan moi eis **hymas***

that was given to me for you,

| 25d | πληρῶσαι τὸν λόγον τοῦ θεοῦ, |
| | *plērōsai ton logon tou theou,* |

to make known to you the word of God in its fullness,

| 26a | τὸ μυστήριον τὸ ἀποκεκρυμμένον |
| | *to mystērion to apokekrymmenon* |

the mystery that has been hidden

| 26b | ἀπὸ τῶν αἰώνων καὶ ἀπὸ τῶν γενεῶν, |
| | *apo tōn aiōnōn kai apo tōn geneōn,* |

for ages and generations,

| 26c | —νῦν δὲ ἐφανερώθη τοῖς ἁγίοις αὐτοῦ, |
| | *—nyn de ephanerōthē tois hagiois autou,* |

but now has been revealed to his saints.

| 27a | οἷς ἠθέλησεν ὁ θεὸς γνωρίσαι |
| | *hois ēthelēsen ho theos gnōrisai* |

To them God chose to make known

| 27b | τί τὸ πλοῦτος τῆς δόξης |
| | *ti to ploutos tēs doxēs* |

| | τοῦ μυστηρίου τούτου ἐν τοῖς ἔθνεσιν, |
| | *tou mystēriou toutou en tois ethnesin,* |

**how great are the riches of the glory
of this mystery among the gentiles,**

| 27c | ὅ ἐστιν Χριστὸς ἐν ὑμῖν, |
| | *ho estin Christos en hymin,* |

which is Christ in you,

| 27d | ἡ ἐλπὶς τῆς δόξης· |
| | *hē elpis tēs doxēs;* |

the hope of glory.

Νῦν χαίρω ἐν τοῖς παθήμασιν ὑπὲρ ὑμῶν,			
Now I rejoice in my sufferings on your behalf,			
Νῦν νῦν	now *Nyn*	---	adv
χαίρω χαίρω	I rejoice *chai·rō*	PRES ACT IND 1ST SG	verb
ἐν ἐν	in *en*	---	prep
τοῖς ὁ	the *tois*	DAT PL NEUT	article
παθήμασιν πάθημα	sufferings/afflictions *pa·thē·ma·sin*	DAT PL NEUT	noun
ὑπὲρ ὑπέρ	on behalf of *hy·per*	---	prep
ὑμῶν σύ	you (all) *hy·mōn*	2ND GEN PL	personal pron

Rejoicing in the midst of trial and suffering is a concept found throughout Paul's epistles. In v. 25 Paul will say that he is a servant of the church, which for Paul means embodying the death, burial, and resurrection life of Christ. This is what it means to participate in the life of Christ in one's own ministry. For Paul, his suffering on behalf of the Colossians means that he is living the cruciform life in Christ in order that the gospel might be made known, that churches such as the one in Colossae may be strengthened, and that believers may also see in him an example of Christlike service. The calling to live this death and resurrection life in Christ on behalf of the Colossians is, for Paul, a reason to rejoice. Paul exemplifies in his own life and ministry the importance of the unity of the body of Christ (1:18) and what it looks like for the church to share in the sufferings of Christ as those who are *in* Christ.

καὶ ἀνταναπληρῶ τὰ ὑστερήματα τῶν θλίψεων τοῦ χριστοῦ			
and I fill up in turn what is lacking in the afflictions of Christ			
καὶ καί	and *kai*	---	conj
ἀνταναπληρῶ ἀνταναπληρόω	I fill up in turn *an·ta·na·plē·rō*	PRES ACT IND 1ST SG	verb
τὰ ὁ	the (things) *ta*	ACC PL NEUT	article
ὑστερήματα ὑστέρημα	lackings *hy·ste·rē·ma·ta*	ACC PL NEUT	noun

τῶν	of the	GEN PL FEM	article
ὁ	*tōn*		
θλίψεων	(of) tribulations/sufferings	GEN PL FEM	noun
θλῖψις	*thli·pse·ōn*		
τοῦ	of the	GEN SG MASC	article
ὁ	*tou*		
χριστοῦ	(of) Christ	GEN SG MASC	noun
Χριστός	*chri·stou*		

The obvious question is how Paul can say there was anything lacking in the afflictions of Christ. Paul here is not referring to Christ's atonement. In fact, **θλῖψις** ("affliction") is never used to describe Christ's suffering on the cross. What Paul is referring to is his active participation in the messianic woes, the suffering that Jews like Paul understood to characterize the time between the two ages, the time when the kingdom of darkness would still be engaged in battle with the kingdom of light. Because he is *in Christ*, as are all Christians, he participates in the suffering of Christ, wherein and through which the gospel is proclaimed during this time *between* the ages. See also Rom 8:17 and Phil 3:10.

24c	**ἐν τῇ σαρκί μου**		
	in my flesh,		
ἐν	in/by/with	---	prep
ἐν	*en*		
τῇ	the	DAT SG FEM	article
ὁ	*tē*		
σαρκί	flesh	DAT SG FEM	noun
σάρξ	*sar·ki*		
μου	of me/my	1ST GEN SG	personal
ἐγώ	*mou*		pron

See also 1:22 for Paul's unusually neutral reference to **σάρξ**.

24d	**ὑπὲρ τοῦ σώματος αὐτοῦ,**		
	for the sake of his body,		
ὑπὲρ	on behalf of/for the sake of	---	prep
ὑπέρ	*hy·per*		
τοῦ	the	GEN SG NEUT	article
ὁ	*tou*		

σώματος	body	GEN SG NEUT	noun
σῶμα	sō·ma·tos		
αὐτοῦ	of him/his	GEN SG MASC	personal
αὐτός	au·tou		pron

24e	ὅ ἐστιν ἡ ἐκκλησία,		
	the church.		
ὅ	which	NOM SG NEUT	relative
ὅς	ho		pron
ἐστιν	(it) is	PRES ACT IND	verb
εἰμί	e·stin	3RD SG	
ἡ	the	NOM SG FEM	article
ὁ	hē		
ἐκκλησία	church	NOM SG FEM	noun
ἐκκλησία	ek·klē·si·a		

Here again is this theme of the church being identified as the body of Christ. It is difficult to overstate just how foundational the notion of participation in Christ was for Paul.

25a	ἧς ἐγενόμην ἐγὼ διάκονος		
	I became its servant		
ἧς	of which	GEN SG FEM	relative
ὅς	hēs		pron
ἐγενόμην	(I) became	AOR MID IND	verb
γίνομαι	e·ge·no·mēn	1ST SG	
ἐγὼ	I	1ST NOM SG	personal
ἐγώ	e·gō		pron
διάκονος	servant/minister	NOM SG MASC	noun
διάκονος	di·a·ko·nos		

25b	κατὰ τὴν οἰκονομίαν τοῦ θεοῦ		
	by God's commission		
κατὰ	according to	---	prep
κατά	ka·ta		

τὴν ὁ	the *tēn*	ACC SG FEM	article
οἰκονομίαν οἰκονομία	stewardship/commission *oi·ko·no·**mi**·an*	ACC SG FEM	noun
τοῦ ὁ	of the *tou*	GEN SG MASC	article
θεοῦ θεός	(of) God *the·**ou***	GEN SG MASC	noun

25c	**τὴν δοθεῖσάν μοι εἰς ὑμᾶς**		
	that was given to me for you,		
τὴν ὁ	the *tēn*	ACC SG FEM	article
δοθεῖσάν δίδωμι	(one) having been given *do·**thei**·san*	AOR PASS PTCP ACC SG FEM	verb
μοι ἐγώ	to me *moi*	1ST DAT SG	personal pron
εἰς εἰς	for *eis*	---	prep
ὑμᾶς σύ	you (all) *hy·**mas***	2ND ACC PL	personal pron

25d	**πληρῶσαι τὸν λόγον τοῦ θεοῦ,**		
	to make known to you the word of God in its fullness,		
πληρῶσαι πληρόω	to fill/fulfill *plē·**rō**·sai*	AOR ACT INF	verb
τὸν ὁ	the *ton*	ACC SG MASC	article
λόγον λόγος	word *lo·gon*	ACC SG MASC	noun
τοῦ ὁ	of the *tou*	GEN SG MASC	article
θεοῦ θεός	(of) God *the·**ou***	GEN SG MASC	noun

Options abound for how to translate **πληρόω** here: "to make the word of God fully known" (ESV, NRSV), "to present to you the word of God in its fullness" (NIV), "to fulfill the word of God" (NKJV). Given Paul's emphasis on the mystery of the gospel in the following verse, it seems he is emphasizing the "completeness" or "fullness" or "complexity" of the gospel itself, rather than the extent to which it is made known.

26a	τὸ μυστήριον τὸ ἀποκεκρυμμένον		
	the mystery that has been hidden		
τὸ ὁ	the *to*	ACC SG NEUT	article
μυστήριον μυστήριον	mystery *my·stē·ri·on*	ACC SG NEUT	noun
τὸ ὁ	the *to*	ACC SG NEUT	article
ἀποκεκρυμμένον ἀποκρύπτω	(one) having been hidden *a·po·ke·krym·me·non*	PERF PASS PTCP ACC SG NEUT	verb

26b	ἀπὸ τῶν αἰώνων καὶ ἀπὸ τῶν γενεῶν,		
	for ages and generations,		
ἀπὸ ἀπό	from *a·po*	---	prep
τῶν ὁ	the *tōn*	GEN PL MASC	article
αἰώνων αἰών	ages *ai·ō·nōn*	GEN PL MASC	noun
καὶ καί	and *kai*	---	conj
ἀπὸ ἀπό	from *a·po*	---	prep
τῶν ὁ	the *tōn*	GEN PL FEM	article
γενεῶν γενεά	generations *ge·ne·ōn*	GEN PL FEM	noun

26c	—νῦν δὲ ἐφανερώθη τοῖς ἁγίοις αὐτοῦ,		
	but now has been revealed to his saints.		
νῦν νῦν	now *nyn*	---	adv

δὲ	but	---	conj
δέ	*de*		
ἐφανερώθη	(it) was manifested/shown	AOR PASS IND	verb
φανερόω	*e·pha·ne·rō·thē*	3RD SG	
τοῖς	to the	DAT PL MASC	article
ὁ	*tois*		
ἁγίοις	(to) holy (ones)/saints	DAT PL MASC	adj
ἅγιος	*ha·gi·ois*		
αὐτοῦ	of him/his	GEN SG MASC	personal
αὐτός	*au·tou*		pron

<table>
<tr><td>27a</td><td colspan="3">οἷς ἠθέλησεν ὁ θεὸς γνωρίσαι</td></tr>
<tr><td colspan="4" align="center">To them God chose to make known</td></tr>
</table>

οἷς	to whom	DAT PL MASC	relative
ὅς	*hois*		pron
ἠθέλησεν	(he) willed	AOR ACT IND	verb
θέλω	*ē·the·lē·sen*	3RD SG	
ὁ	the	NOM SG MASC	article
ὁ	*ho*		
θεὸς	God	NOM SG MASC	noun
θεός	*the·os*		
γνωρίσαι	to make known	AOR ACT INF	verb
γνωρίζω	*gnō·ri·sai*		

<table>
<tr><td>27b</td><td colspan="3" align="center">τί τὸ πλοῦτος τῆς δόξης
τοῦ μυστηρίου τούτου ἐν τοῖς ἔθνεσιν,</td></tr>
<tr><td colspan="4" align="center">how great are the riches of the glory
of this mystery among the gentiles,</td></tr>
</table>

τί	what?	NOM SG NEUT	interr
τίς	*ti*		pron
τὸ	the	NOM SG NEUT	article
ὁ	*to*		
πλοῦτος	riches	NOM SG NEUT	noun
πλοῦτος	*plou·tos*		
τῆς	of the	GEN SG FEM	article
ὁ	*tēs*		
δόξης	(of) glory	GEN SG FEM	noun
δόξα	*do·xēs*		

τοῦ	of the	GEN SG NEUT	article
ὁ	*tou*		
μυστηρίου	(of) mystery	GEN SG NEUT	noun
μυστήριον	*my·stē·ri·ou*		
τούτου	of this	GEN SG NEUT	demonstr
οὗτος	*tou·tou*		pron
ἐν	in/among	---	prep
ἐν	*en*		
τοῖς	the	DAT PL NEUT	article
ὁ	*tois*		
ἔθνεσιν	gentiles/nations	DAT PL NEUT	noun
ἔθνος	*eth·ne·sin*		

27c	**ὅ ἐστιν Χριστὸς ἐν ὑμῖν,**
	which is Christ in you,

ὅ	which	NOM SG NEUT	relative
ὅς	*ho*		pron
ἐστιν	(it) is	PRES ACT IND	verb
εἰμί	*e·stin*	3RD SG	
Χριστὸς	Christ	NOM SG MASC	noun
Χριστός	*Chri·stos*		
ἐν	in/by/with	---	prep
ἐν	*en*		
ὑμῖν	you	2ND DAT PL	personal
σύ	*hy·min*		pron

The mystery is this: from eternity ("ages"), God divinely intended to bring the gentiles into his family through the person and work of the Messiah. Those *in Christ* would be *in* the family of God. And yet, part of that remarkable mystery is that God always intended to transform the individual by the indwelling of Christ *in* the believer through the indwelling of the Holy Spirit. Notice that Paul uses a plural personal pronoun: **ὑμῖν**. He is speaking to the corporate body of believers in Colossae. It is this indwelling of Christ by the Holy Spirit which creates the "body of Christ." Yet, Paul would not exclude the individual believer from this indwelling.

ἡ ἐλπὶς τῆς δόξης·

the hope of glory.

ἡ ὁ	the *hē*	NOM SG FEM	article
ἐλπὶς ἐλπίς	hope *el·pis*	NOM SG FEM	noun
τῆς ὁ	of the *tēs*	GEN SG FEM	article
δόξης δόξα	(of) glory *do·xēs*	GEN SG FEM	noun

This indwelling of Christ in the gentiles, this mystery of God kept hidden, and not any other honor or aspiration, is purest glory. See also 1 Cor 2:6–7. The revelation of this mystery is part and parcel of Paul's apocalyptic theology, wherein he sees God breaking into the present evil age (Gal 1:4) to reveal (**ἀποκαλύπτω**, Eph 3:4–5) the mystery that God has kept hidden from eternity. Here Paul is emphasizing the inclusion of the gentiles as the aspect of that mystery that was formerly hidden and is now "revealed." Paul does not use "reveal" here, but **γνωρίσαι** ("to make known," 1:27a), which carries the same effect.

28a ὃν ἡμεῖς καταγγέλλομεν

hon hēmeis katangellomen

We proclaim him,

28b νουθετοῦντες πάντα ἄνθρωπον

nouthetountes panta anthrōpon

admonishing everyone

28c καὶ διδάσκοντες πάντα ἄνθρωπον ἐν πάσῃ σοφίᾳ,

kai didaskontes panta anthrōpon en pasē sophia,

and teaching everyone with all wisdom,

28d ἵνα παραστήσωμεν πάντα ἄνθρωπον τέλειον ἐν Χριστῷ·

hina parastēsōmen panta anthrōpon teleion en Christō;

that we might present everyone mature in Christ.

29a εἰς ὃ καὶ κοπιῶ

eis ho kai kopiō

For this I toil,

29b ἀγωνιζόμενος κατὰ τὴν ἐνέργειαν αὐτοῦ

agōnizomenos kata tēn energeian autou

τὴν ἐνεργουμένην ἐν ἐμοὶ ἐν δυνάμει.

tēn energoumenēn en emoi en dynamei.

struggling with his energy that powerfully works within me.

ὃν ἡμεῖς καταγγέλλομεν

We proclaim him,

ὃν	which	ACC SG MASC	relative
ὅς	*hon*		pron
ἡμεῖς	we	1ST NOM PL	personal
ἐγώ	*hē·meis*		pron
καταγγέλλομεν	(we) declare/proclaim	PRES ACT IND	verb
καταγγέλλω	*kat·an·gel·lo·men*	1ST PL	

Paul switches from the first-person singular (1:24–25) to a first-person plural here, emphasizing the role of Timothy and others.

νουθετοῦντες πάντα ἄνθρωπον

admonishing everyone

νουθετοῦντες	admonishing/exhorting	PRES ACT PTCP	verb
νουθετέω	*nou·the·toun·tes*	NOM PL MASC	
πάντα	each/every/all	ACC SG MASC	adj
πᾶς	*pan·ta*		
ἄνθρωπον	man/person	ACC SG MASC	noun
ἄνθρωπος	*an·thrō·pon*		

καὶ διδάσκοντες πάντα ἄνθρωπον ἐν πάσῃ σοφίᾳ,

and teaching everyone with all wisdom,

καὶ	and	---	conj
καί	*kai*		
διδάσκοντες	(those) teaching	PRES ACT PTCP	verb
διδάσκω	*di·da·skon·tes*	NOM PL MASC	
πάντα	each/every/all	ACC SG MASC	adj
πᾶς	*pan·ta*		
ἄνθρωπον	man/person	ACC SG MASC	noun
ἄνθρωπος	*an·thrō·pon*		
ἐν	in/by/with	---	prep
ἐν	*en*		
πάσῃ	each/every/all	DAT SG FEM	adj
πᾶς	*pa·sē*		
σοφίᾳ	wisdom	DAT SG FEM	noun
σοφία	*so·phi·a*		

28d	ἵνα παραστήσωμεν πάντα ἄνθρωπον τέλειον ἐν Χριστῷ·

that we might present everyone mature in Christ.

ἵνα ἵνα	that/in order that *hi·na*	---	conj
παραστήσωμεν παρίστημι	we might present *pa·ra·stē·sō·men*	AOR ACT SUBJ 1ST PL	verb
πάντα πᾶς	each/every/all *pan·ta*	ACC SG MASC	adj
ἄνθρωπον ἄνθρωπος	man/person *an·thrō·pon*	ACC SG MASC	noun
τέλειον τέλειος	mature/complete *te·lei·on*	ACC SG MASC	adj
ἐν ἐν	in/by/with *en*	---	prep
Χριστῷ Χριστός	Christ *Chri·stō*	DAT SG MASC	noun

In 1:28 Paul writes **πάντα ἄνθρωπον** ("everyone") three times, reiterating the cosmic inclusivity of the gospel. This is the goal of salvation for Paul: maturity in Christ (or, as he writes in Rom 8:29, "conformity" to Christ). Those who are *in* Christ, then, need to have that identity brought to a point of maturity or completeness. This comes through living a life in faithfulness to Christ and worthy of the gospel of Christ (Col 1:10)—Paul's initial point in the letter.

29a	εἰς ὃ καὶ κοπιῶ

For this I toil,

εἰς εἰς	into/for *eis*	---	prep
ὃ ὅς	which *ho*	ACC SG NEUT	relative pron
καὶ καί	and/also/even *kai*	---	conj
κοπιῶ κοπιάω	I labor/toil *ko·pi·ō*	PRES ACT IND 1ST SG	verb

ἀγωνιζόμενος κατὰ τὴν ἐνέργειαν αὐτοῦ τὴν ἐνεργουμένην ἐν ἐμοὶ ἐν δυνάμει.

struggling with his energy
that powerfully works within me.

ἀγωνιζόμενος ἀγωνίζομαι	fighting/struggling *a·gō·ni·zo·me·nos*	PRES MID PTCP NOM SG MASC	verb
κατὰ κατά	according to/against *ka·ta*	---	prep
τὴν ὁ	the *tēn*	ACC SG FEM	article
ἐνέργειαν ἐνέργεια	power/energy *en·er·gei·an*	ACC SG FEM	noun
αὐτοῦ αὐτός	of him/his *au·tou*	GEN SG MASC	personal pron
τὴν ὁ	the *tēn*	ACC SG FEM	article
ἐνεργουμένην ἐνεργέω	(one) working in *en·er·gou·me·nēn*	PRES MID PTCP ACC SG FEM	verb
ἐν ἐν	in/by/with *en*	---	prep
ἐμοὶ ἐγώ	me *e·moi*	1ST DAT SG	personal pron
ἐν ἐν	in/by/with *en*	---	prep
δυνάμει δύναμις	power *dy·na·mei*	DAT SG FEM	noun

As Paul will tell us in 2:12, this "energy" (ἐνέργεια) that works in Paul is the same ἐνέργεια that God used to raise Jesus from the dead.

1a Θέλω γὰρ ὑμᾶς εἰδέναι ἡλίκον ἀγῶνα ἔχω ὑπὲρ ὑμῶν

Thelō gar hymas eidenai hēlikon agōna echō hyper hymōn

For I want you to know much I am struggling for you

1b καὶ τῶν ἐν Λαοδικίᾳ

kai tōn en Laodikia

and those in Laodicea

1c καὶ ὅσοι οὐχ ἑόρακαν τὸ πρόσωπόν μου ἐν σαρκί,

kai hosoi ouch heorakan to prosōpon mou en sarki,

and for all who have not seen me face to face,

2a ἵνα παρακληθῶσιν αἱ καρδίαι αὐτῶν,

hina paraklēthōsin hai kardiai autōn,

in order that their hearts would be encouraged,

2b συνβιβασθέντες ἐν ἀγάπῃ

synbibasthentes en agapē

held together in love,

2c καὶ εἰς πᾶν πλοῦτος

kai eis pan ploutos

τῆς πληροφορίας τῆς συνέσεως,

tēs plērophorias tēs syneseōs,

**and that they may have all the riches
of full assurance of understanding,**

2d εἰς ἐπίγνωσιν τοῦ μυστηρίου τοῦ θεοῦ, Χριστοῦ,

eis epignōsin tou mystēriou tou theou, Christou,

that they may fully know the mystery of God, namely, Christ,

3   ἐν ᾧ εἰσὶν πάντες οἱ θησαυροὶ

en hō eisin pantes hoi thēsauroi

τῆς σοφίας καὶ γνώσεως ἀπόκρυφοι.

tēs sophias kai gnōseōs apokryphoi.

in whom are hidden all the treasures of wisdom and knowledge.

1a	Θέλω γὰρ ὑμᾶς εἰδέναι ἡλίκον ἀγῶνα ἔχω ὑπὲρ ὑμῶν		
	For I want you to know much I am struggling for you		
Θέλω	I will/wish	PRES ACT IND	verb
θέλω	*The·lō*	1ST SG	
γὰρ	for/because	---	conj
γάρ	*gar*		
ὑμᾶς	you (all)	2ND ACC PL	personal
σύ	*hy·mas*		pron
εἰδέναι	to have known	PERF ACT INF	verb
εἰδώ	*ei·de·nai*		
ἡλίκον	how great	ACC SG MASC	adj
ἡλίκος	*hē·li·kon*		
ἀγῶνα	struggle	ACC SG MASC	noun
ἀγών	*a·gō·na*		
ἔχω	I have	PRES ACT IND	verb
ἔχω	*e·chō*	1ST SG	
ὑπὲρ	on behalf of	---	prep
ὑπέρ	*hy·per*		
ὑμῶν	you (all)	2ND GEN PL	personal
σύ	*hy·mōn*		pron

1b	καὶ τῶν ἐν Λαοδικίᾳ		
	and those in Laodicea		
καὶ	and	---	conj
καί	*kai*		
τῶν	of the ones	GEN PL MASC	article
ὁ	*tōn*		

ἐν	in	---	prep
ἐν	*en*		
Λαοδικίᾳ	Laodicea	DAT SG FEM	noun
Λαοδίκεια	*La·o·di·ki·a*		

1c	**καὶ ὅσοι οὐχ ἑόρακαν τὸ πρόσωπόν μου ἐν σαρκί,**
	and for all who have not seen me face to face,

καὶ	and	---	conj
καί	*kai*		
ὅσοι	as many as	NOM PL MASC	correlative
ὅσος	*ho·soi*		pron
οὐχ	no/not	---	particle
οὐ	*ouch*		
ἑόρακαν	(they) have seen	PERF ACT IND	verb
ὁράω	*he·o·ra·kan*	3RD PL	
τὸ	the	ACC SG NEUT	article
ὁ	*to*		
πρόσωπόν	face	ACC SG NEUT	noun
πρόσωπον	*pro·sō·pon*		
μου	of me/my	1ST GEN SG	personal
ἐγώ	*mou*		pron
ἐν	in	---	prep
ἐν	*en*		
σαρκί	flesh	DAT SG FEM	noun
σάρξ	*sar·ki*		

This is the third time Paul has used **σάρξ** as a neutral word to describe a physical body, rather than with negative connotations that elevate it to an evil power at work in the world (i.e., "Flesh"; see, e.g., Gal 5:17).

2a	**ἵνα παρακληθῶσιν αἱ καρδίαι αὐτῶν,**
	in order that their hearts would be encouraged,

ἵνα	that/in order that	---	conj
ἵνα	*hi·na*		
παρακληθῶσιν	(they) might be comforted/ encouraged	AOR PASS SUBJ 3RD PL	verb
παρακαλέω	*pa·ra·klē·thō·sin*		
αἱ	the	NOM PL FEM	article
ὁ	*hai*		

καρδίαι	hearts	NOM PL FEM	noun
καρδία	*kar·di·ai*		
αὐτῶν	of them	GEN PL MASC	personal
αὐτός	*au·tōn*		pron

2b	συνβιβασθέντες ἐν ἀγάπῃ		
	held together in love,		
συνβιβασθέντες	(those) having been united	AOR PASS PTCP	verb
συμβιβάζω	*syn·bi·ba·sthen·tes*	NOM PL MASC	
ἐν	in/by/with	---	prep
ἐν	*en*		
ἀγάπῃ	love	DAT SG FEM	noun
ἀγάπη	*a·ga·pē*		

2c	καὶ εἰς πᾶν πλοῦτος τῆς πληροφορίας τῆς συνέσεως,		
	and that they may have all the riches of full assurance of understanding,		
καὶ	and	---	conj
καί	*kai*		
εἰς	into/for	---	prep
εἰς	*eis*		
πᾶν	all	ACC SG NEUT	adj
πᾶς	*pan*		
πλοῦτος	riches/wealth	ACC SG NEUT	noun
πλοῦτος	*plou·tos*		
τῆς	of the	GEN SG FEM	article
ὁ	*tēs*		
πληροφορίας	(of) full assurance/certainty	GEN SG FEM	noun
πληροφορία	*plē·ro·pho·ri·as*		
τῆς	of the	GEN SG FEM	article
ὁ	*tēs*		
συνέσεως	(of) understanding/insight	GEN SG FEM	noun
σύνεσις	*syn·e·se·ōs*		

εἰς ἐπίγνωσιν τοῦ μυστηρίου τοῦ θεοῦ, Χριστοῦ,

that they may fully know the mystery of God, namely, Christ,

εἰς εἰς	into/for *eis*	---	prep
ἐπίγνωσιν ἐπίγνωσις	full knowledge *e·pi·gnō·sin*	ACC SG FEM	noun
τοῦ ὁ	of the ***tou***	GEN SG NEUT	article
μυστηρίου μυστήριον	(of) mystery *my·stē·ri·ou*	GEN SG NEUT	noun
τοῦ ὁ	of the ***tou***	GEN SG MASC	article
θεοῦ θεός	(of) God *the·ou*	GEN SG MASC	noun
Χριστοῦ Χριστός	(of) Christ *Chri·stou*	GEN SG MASC	noun

More than any spiritual battle or divine warfare, the fundamental element of Jewish apocalyptic texts, which Paul has clearly been influenced by, is God's revelation of hidden knowledge. Here Paul says that the mystery that God kept hidden for eternity (1:26) and that he has now revealed is the Messiah himself.

ἐν ᾧ εἰσὶν πάντες οἱ θησαυροὶ τῆς σοφίας καὶ γνώσεως ἀπόκρυφοι.

in whom are hidden all the treasures of wisdom and knowledge.

ἐν ἐν	in *en*	---	prep
ᾧ ὅς	whom ***hō***	DAT SG MASC	relative pron
εἰσὶν εἰμί	(they) are *ei·sin*	PRES ACT IND 3RD PL	verb
πάντες πᾶς	all (ones) ***pan·tes***	NOM PL MASC	adj
οἱ ὁ	the *hoi*	NOM PL MASC	article
θησαυροὶ θησαυρός	treasures *thē·sau·roi*	NOM PL MASC	noun
τῆς ὁ	of the *tēs*	GEN SG FEM	article

σοφίας σοφία	(of) wisdom *so·**phi**·as*	GEN SG FEM	noun
καὶ καί	and ***kai***	---	conj
γνώσεως γνῶσις	(of) knowledge ***gnō**·se·ōs*	GEN SG FEM	noun
ἀπόκρυφοι ἀπόκρυφος	secret/hidden (ones) *a·**po**·kry·phoi*	NOM PL MASC	adj

How are these divine mysteries revealed? Not through apocalyptic visions, as in Daniel or Ezekiel, or through being carried away to a heavenly realm, as in Revelation, but in Jesus Christ himself.

4a
Τοῦτο λέγω

Touto legō

I say this

4b
ἵνα μηδεὶς ὑμᾶς παραλογίζηται ἐν πιθανολογίᾳ.

hina mēdeis hymas paralogizētai en pithanologia.

in order that no one might deceive you with enticing arguments.

5a
εἰ γὰρ καὶ τῇ σαρκὶ ἄπειμι,

ei gar kai tē sarki apeimi,

For even though I am absent in body,

5b
ἀλλὰ τῷ πνεύματι σὺν ὑμῖν εἰμί,

alla tō pneumati syn hymin eimi,

I am still with you in spirit,

5c
χαίρων καὶ βλέπων ὑμῶν τὴν τάξιν

chairōn kai blepōn hymōn tēn taxin

and I rejoice to see how disciplined you are

5d
καὶ τὸ στερέωμα τῆς εἰς Χριστὸν πίστεως ὑμῶν.

kai to stereōma tēs eis Christon pisteōs hymōn.

and how firm your faith in Christ is.

4a	**Τοῦτο λέγω**		
	I say this		
Τοῦτο	this	ACC SG NEUT	demonstr
οὗτος	*Tou·to*		pron

| λέγω | I say | PRES ACT IND | verb |
| λέγω | *le·gō* | 1ST SG | |

ἵνα μηδεὶς ὑμᾶς παραλογίζηται ἐν πιθανολογίᾳ.

in order that no one might deceive you with enticing arguments.

ἵνα	that/in order that	---	conj
ἵνα	*hi·na*		
μηδεὶς	no one	NOM SG MASC	adj
μηδείς	*mē·deis*		
ὑμᾶς	you (all)	2ND ACC PL	personal
σύ	*hy·mas*		pron
παραλογίζηται	(he) might deceive	PRES MID SUBJ	verb
παραλογίζομαι	*pa·ra·lo·gi·zē·tai*	3RD SG	
ἐν	by/with	---	prep
ἐν	*en*		
πιθανολογίᾳ	enticing argument	DAT SG FEM	noun
πιθανολογία	*pi·tha·no·lo·gi·a*		

We can translate **πιθανολογίᾳ** here in multiple ways: "plausible" (ESV, NRSV), "fine-sounding" (NIV), "persuasive" (NKJV), "beguiling" (RSV).

εἰ γὰρ καὶ τῇ σαρκὶ ἄπειμι,

For even though I am absent in body,

εἰ	if	---	cond
εἰ	*ei*		
γὰρ	for	---	conj
γάρ	*gar*		
καὶ	and/also/even	---	conj
καί	*kai*		
τῇ	in the	DAT SG FEM	article
ὁ	*tē*		
σαρκὶ	(in) flesh	DAT SG FEM	noun
σάρξ	*sar·ki*		
ἄπειμι	I am away/absent	PRES ACT IND 1ST SG	verb
ἄπειμι	*ap·ei·mi*		

For the fourth time, Paul emphasizes physical presence with the use of **σάρξ**.

ἀλλὰ τῷ πνεύματι σὺν ὑμῖν εἰμί,

I am still with you in spirit,

ἀλλὰ	but	---	conj
ἀλλά	*al·la*		
τῷ	to the	DAT SG NEUT	article
ὁ	*tō*		
πνεύματι	(in) spirit	DAT SG NEUT	noun
πνεῦμα	*pneu·ma·ti*		
σὺν	with	---	prep
σύν	*syn*		
ὑμῖν	you (all)	2ND DAT PL	personal
σύ	*hy·min*		pron
εἰμί	I am	PRES ACT IND	verb
εἰμί	*ei·mi*	1ST SG	

χαίρων καὶ βλέπων ὑμῶν τὴν τάξιν

and I rejoice to see how disciplined you are

χαίρων	(I) am rejoicing	PRES ACT PTCP	verb
χαίρω	*chai·rōn*	NOM SG MASC	
καὶ	and	---	conj
καί	*kai*		
βλέπων	(I) am seeing/looking	PRES ACT PTCP	verb
βλέπω	*ble·pōn*	NOM SG MASC	
ὑμῶν	of you (all)/your	2ND GEN PL	personal
σύ	*hy·mōn*		pron
τὴν	the	ACC SG FEM	article
ὁ	*tēn*		
τάξιν	order/arrangement	ACC SG FEM	noun
τάξις	*ta·xin*		

καὶ τὸ στερέωμα τῆς εἰς Χριστὸν πίστεως ὑμῶν.

and how firm your faith in Christ is.

καὶ	and	---	conj
καί	*kai*		
τὸ	the	ACC SG NEUT	article
ὁ	*to*		
στερέωμα	firmness	ACC SG NEUT	noun
στερέωμα	*ste·re·ō·ma*		

τῆς	of the	GEN SG FEM	article
ὁ	*tēs*		
εἰς	into/for	---	prep
εἰς	*eis*		
Χριστὸν	Christ	ACC SG MASC	noun
Χριστός	*Chri·ston*		
πίστεως	(of) faith	GEN SG FEM	noun
πίστις	*pi·ste·ōs*		
ὑμῶν	of you (all)	2ND GEN PL	personal
σύ	*hy·mōn*		pron

6a   Ὡς οὖν παρελάβετε τὸν χριστὸν Ἰησοῦν τὸν κύριον,

   *Hōs **oun** parelabete **ton** christon Iēsoun **ton** kyrion,*

Therefore, just as you received Christ Jesus as Lord,

6b   ἐν αὐτῷ περιπατεῖτε,

    en autō peripateite,

continue to live out your lives in him,

7a   ἐρριζωμένοι καὶ ἐποικοδομούμενοι ἐν αὐτῷ

   *errhizōmenoi **kai** epoikodomoumenoi en autō*

having been rooted and built up in him

7b   καὶ βεβαιούμενοι τῇ πίστει

    ***kai** bebaioumenoi **tē** pistei*

and established in the faith,

7c   καθὼς ἐδιδάχθητε,

    kathōs edidachthēte,

just as you were taught,

7d   περισσεύοντες ἐν εὐχαριστίᾳ.

    perisseuontes en eucharistia.

abounding in thanksgiving.

6a	Ὡς οὖν παρελάβετε τὸν χριστὸν Ἰησοῦν τὸν κύριον,		
	Therefore, just as you received Christ Jesus as Lord,		
Ὡς	as	---	adv
ὡς	*Hōs*		

οὖν οὖν	therefore *oun*	---	conj
παρελάβετε παραλαμβάνω	you (all) received/took *par·e·**la**·be·te*	AOR ACT IND 2ND PL	verb
τὸν ὁ	the *ton*	ACC SG MASC	article
χριστὸν Χριστός	Christ *chri·**ston***	ACC SG MASC	noun
Ἰησοῦν Ἰησοῦς	Jesus *I·ē·**soun***	ACC SG MASC	noun
τὸν ὁ	the *ton*	ACC SG MASC	article
κύριον κύριος	Lord *ky·ri·on*	ACC SG MASC	noun

6b	**ἐν αὐτῷ περιπατεῖτε,**

continue to live out your lives in him,

ἐν ἐν	in/by/with *en*	---	prep
αὐτῷ αὐτός	him *au·tō*	DAT SG MASC	personal pron
περιπατεῖτε περιπατέω	(you all) walk *pe·ri·pa·**tei**·te*	PRES ACT IMPV 2ND PL	verb

---

7a	**ἐρριζωμένοι καὶ ἐποικοδομούμενοι ἐν αὐτῷ**

having been rooted and built up in him

ἐρριζωμένοι ῥιζόω	having been rooted/ strengthened *er·rhi·zō·**me**·noi*	PERF PASS PTCP NOM PL MASC	verb
καὶ καί	and *kai*	---	conj
ἐποικοδομούμενοι ἐποικοδομέω	being built upon *ep·oi·ko·do·**mou**·me·noi*	PRES PASS PTCP NOM PL MASC	verb
ἐν ἐν	in/by/with *en*	---	prep
αὐτῷ αὐτός	him *au·tō*	DAT SG MASC	personal pron

Paul takes his readers back full circle to his prayer for them in 1:10: that they would "walk" their lives in a manner worthy of the gospel. Their truest identity is *in* Christ. They are "rooted" in him. The word ῥιζόω ("to take root") here is used only one other time in the New Testament (Eph 3:17) and only five times in the Septuagint (Sir 3:28; 24:12; Pss. Sol. 14:4; Isa 40:24; Jer 12:2). In most Septuagintal uses, the metaphor is that of a plant taking root in the soil. The Colossian Christians are planted in Christ, have taken root in Christ, and are now being built up in Christ.

7b	καὶ βεβαιούμενοι τῇ πίστει		
	and established in the faith,		
καὶ καί	and ***kai***	---	conj
βεβαιούμενοι βεβαιόω	being confirmed/ established *be·bai·**ou**·me·noi*	PRES PASS PTCP NOM PL MASC	verb
τῇ ὁ	in the ***tē***	DAT SG FEM	article
πίστει πίστις	faith ***pi***·*stei*	DAT SG FEM	noun

7c	καθὼς ἐδιδάχθητε,		
	just as you were taught,		
καθὼς καθώς	just as *ka·**thōs***	---	adv
ἐδιδάχθητε διδάσκω	you (all) were taught *e·di·**dach**·thē·te*	AOR PASS IND 2ND PL	verb

7d	περισσεύοντες ἐν εὐχαριστίᾳ.		
	abounding in thanksgiving.		
περισσεύοντες περισσεύω	abounding *pe·ris·**seu**·on·tes*	PRES ACT PTCP NOM PL MASC	verb
ἐν ἐν	in/with *en*	---	prep
εὐχαριστίᾳ εὐχαριστία	thanksgiving *eu·cha·ri·**sti**·a*	DAT SG FEM	noun

🌱 *Big Idea.* Pastoral ministry includes suffering, struggling, and contending on behalf of believers, pointing them to the mystery of God in Christ, in order that they might become spiritually mature in Christ.

🌱 *Bridge to Theology.* In contrast to the previous emphasis on cosmological warfare, Paul's emphases now feel rather mundane. And yet, it is his ministerial relationship with the Colossians that forms the pastoral heart of this letter. He describes how he is contending or struggling for the Colossians in his ministry, praying that they would grow in the wisdom and knowledge of Christ, who is the mystery of God (1:26–27; 2:2). Part of Paul's early Jewish apocalyptic framework is the idea that God kept secrets or mysteries that were only revealed to seers or prophets. Sometimes these mysteries were revealed in visions, as in the book of Daniel. According to Paul, though, the mystery of God is revealed to all people in Christ; Jesus is the mystery of God "in whom are hidden all the treasures of wisdom and knowledge" (2:3). It is this wisdom and knowledge that leads a person to maturity in Christ (1:28) and whereby they learn to discern when an argument is truly from God or whether it is intended to deceive. Here Paul sets the context for the next passage, where he will challenge the Colossian believers not to be persuaded by the "Colossian heresy."

🌱 *Illustrations/Applications.* The implicit challenge to grow in the wisdom and knowledge of Christ, which leads to spiritual maturity, is perhaps one of the most difficult challenges of the entire letter. It's much easier said than done, and, as many know, it takes a lifetime of intentionality. There are several directions in which you might go when preaching this.

One direction might be to encourage your congregants to study the perspectives of culture and society on topics that occupy many news outlets—e.g., politics, finances, the environment, and so on, or topics like leadership, service, diversity and equity, race, gender, etc. Can you recommend a few books or articles or podcasts to those who are interested to learn what the Bible says in relation to what culture says?

Another direction might be to encourage intentional activism in pursuing the wisdom of Christ in applied ministry. That is, we discern the wisdom and knowledge of Christ through practical ministry: e.g., serving at a homeless shelter, volunteering at a neighborhood high school, or working side by side with people who are differently abled than ourselves.

The wisdom and knowledge of Christ surely is more easily discerned in these contexts than it is from reading a textbook.

Perhaps the balance to this would be pursuing the wisdom and knowledge of Christ in the biblical text itself. Biblical literacy is on the decline. In my experience as a Bible professor at an undergraduate Christian liberal arts institution, I would go so far as to say that biblical literacy is no longer regular—it is rare. Can you challenge your congregants to study Scripture, to learn the grand narrative of the text, to think critically about creation, sin, exile, and redemption themes throughout the text, and to learn to see the ways in which God's faithfulness to his Old Testament promises is evident throughout the New Testament writings, and of course, in Jesus Christ himself? Perhaps an able teacher in the church could lead a few special study sessions, or your small group ministry might focus on learning these biblical themes together.

A NEW IDENTITY IN CHRIST

If the Colossian Christians need to be reminded of just one thing, it is this: their life is no longer defined by their participation in the kingdom of darkness, living as enemies of God, doing evil, and having their sins count against them. That is no longer who they are. Instead, their truest identity, even if it is not always obvious, is that of Christ himself. They are in Christ. They have been circumcised by Christ, baptized into Christ, and made alive with Christ. What is true of him is true of them. They need only to live out that reality. This is the heart of Paul's message to the Colossians.

8a
Βλέπετε μή τις ὑμᾶς ἔσται ὁ συλαγωγῶν

Blepete mē tis hymas estai ho sylagōgōn

See to it that no one takes you captive

8b
διὰ τῆς φιλοσοφίας

dia tēs philosophias

through philosophy

8c
καὶ κενῆς ἀπάτης

kai kenēs apatēs

and empty deceit,

8d
κατὰ τὴν παράδοσιν τῶν ἀνθρώπων,

kata tēn paradosin tōn anthrōpōn,

according to human tradition,

8e
κατὰ τὰ στοιχεῖα τοῦ κόσμου

kata ta stoicheia tou kosmou

according to the elemental spirits of the world,

8f
καὶ οὐ κατὰ Χριστόν·

kai ou kata Christon;

and not according to Christ.

9
ὅτι ἐν αὐτῷ κατοικεῖ πᾶν τὸ πλήρωμα τῆς θεότητος σωματικῶς,

hoti en autō katoikei pan to plērōma tēs theotētos sōmatikōs,

For in him all the fullness of deity dwells in bodily form,

10a
καὶ ἐστὲ ἐν αὐτῷ πεπληρωμένοι,

kai este en autō peplērōmenoi,

and you have been brought to fullness in him,

ὅς ἐστιν ἡ κεφαλὴ πάσης ἀρχῆς καὶ ἐξουσίας,

hos estin hē kephalē pasēs archēs kai exousias,

who is the head over every ruler and authority.

8a	Βλέπετε μή τις ὑμᾶς ἔσται ὁ συλαγωγῶν		
	See to it that no one takes you captive		
Βλέπετε βλέπω	(you all) see/look *Ble·pe·te*	PRES ACT IMPV 2ND PL	verb
μή μή	not/no *mē*	---	particle
τις τίς	someone/anyone *tis*	NOM SG MASC	indef pron
ὑμᾶς σύ	you (all) *hy·mas*	2ND ACC PL	personal pron
ἔσται εἰμί	he/she/it will be *e·stai*	FUT MID IND 3RD SG	verb
ὁ ὁ	the *ho*	NOM SG MASC	article
συλαγωγῶν συλαγωγέω	(one) making captive *sy·la·gō·gōn*	PRES ACT PTCP NOM SG MASC	verb

Paul transitions here to at least one reason for writing the letter—some form of erroneous teaching that is spreading or has the possibility of spreading throughout the church in Colossae. For a helpful introduction to what this teaching might have been, see Michael Bird's highly accessible commentary *Colossians and Philemon* (2009). The word Paul uses here is the indefinite **τις** ("someone/anyone"), which refers only generally to someone/anyone; but it's also quite possible and even likely that he has a particular individual in mind and is writing about that person in a generalized manner.

8b	**διὰ τῆς φιλοσοφίας**		
	through philosophy		
διὰ διά	through di·a	---	prep
τῆς ὁ	the tēs	GEN SG FEM	article
φιλοσοφίας φιλοσοφία	philosophy phi·lo·so·phi·as	GEN SG FEM	noun

8c	**καὶ κενῆς ἀπάτης**		
	and empty deceit,		
καὶ καί	and kai	---	conj
κενῆς κενός	of empty/vain ke·nēs	GEN SG FEM	adj
ἀπάτης ἀπάτη	deceit a·pa·tēs	GEN SG FEM	noun

The **καὶ** ("and") in this case is likely epexegetical, meaning that the "empty deceit" (**κενῆς ἀπάτης**) is a restatement and elaboration of the "philosophy" (**φιλοσοφίας**): "through deceitful and empty philosophy." Additionally, **φιλοσοφία** here does not refer to philosophy in general or particular philosophies or philosophers, such as Aristotle. Rather, given the inclusion of the article (**τῆς φιλοσοφίας**) that renders it "*the* philosophy," it more likely refers to the teaching that is being spread in Colossae and which is being used to "take captive" the Colossian Christians. Suffice it to say here that it is likely a syncretism of traditional Jewish beliefs (about the Sabbath, Torah, and festivals) and Hellenistic beliefs (emphasizing angels and spiritual powers).

8d	**κατὰ τὴν παράδοσιν τῶν ἀνθρώπων,**		
	according to human tradition,		
κατὰ κατά	according to ka·ta	---	prep
τὴν ὁ	the tēn	ACC SG FEM	article
παράδοσιν παράδοσις	tradition pa·ra·do·sin	ACC SG FEM	noun

τῶν	of the	GEN PL MASC	article
ὁ	*tōn*		
ἀνθρώπων	(of) people	GEN PL MASC	noun
ἄνθρωπος	*an·thrō·pōn*		

8e	**κατὰ τὰ στοιχεῖα τοῦ κόσμου**		
	according to the elemental spirits of the world,		
κατὰ	according to	---	prep
κατά	*ka·ta*		
τὰ	the	ACC PL NEUT	article
ὁ	*ta*		
στοιχεῖα	elements/elementary principles	ACC PL NEUT	noun
στοιχεῖον	*stoi·chei·a*		
τοῦ	of the	GEN SG MASC	article
ὁ	*tou*		
κόσμου	(of) world/universe	GEN SG MASC	noun
κόσμος	*ko·smou*		

Στοιχεῖα ("elemental spirits") here and elsewhere (esp. Gal 4:3, 9) likely refers to the same ruling angelic powers Paul mentioned in Col 1:16 and will mention again in 2:15. These rulers and powers are those that serve the kingdom of darkness in which we formerly participated and from which we were rescued (1:13) and redeemed (1:14).

8f	**καὶ οὐ κατὰ Χριστόν·**		
	and not according to Christ.		
καὶ	and	---	conj
καί	*kai*		
οὐ	not	---	particle
οὐ	*ou*		
κατὰ	according to	---	prep
κατά	*ka·ta*		
Χριστόν	Christ	ACC SG MASC	noun
Χριστός	*Chri·ston*		

ὅτι ἐν αὐτῷ κατοικεῖ πᾶν τὸ πλήρωμα τῆς θεότητος σωματικῶς,

For in him all the fullness of deity dwells in bodily form,

ὅτι ὅτι	because/since *ho·ti*	- - -	conj
ἐν ἐν	in/by/with *en*	- - -	prep
αὐτῷ αὐτός	him *au·tō*	DAT SG MASC	personal pron
κατοικεῖ κατοικέω	(it) dwells *kat·oi·kei*	PRES ACT IND 3RD SG	verb
πᾶν πᾶς	all *pan*	NOM SG NEUT	adj
τὸ ὁ	the *to*	NOM SG NEUT	article
πλήρωμα πλήρωμα	fullness *plē·rō·ma*	NOM SG NEUT	noun
τῆς ὁ	of the *tēs*	GEN SG FEM	article
θεότητος θεότης	(of) deity *the·o·tē·tos*	GEN SG FEM	noun
σωματικῶς σωματικῶς	in bodily form *sō·ma·ti·kōs*	- - -	adv

Paul returns to the christological themes established in 1:15–20, here emphasizing the visible, bodily existence of God in Christ that he wrote about in 1:15.

10a		**καὶ ἐστὲ ἐν αὐτῷ πεπληρωμένοι,**	

and you have been brought to fullness in him,

καὶ καί	and *kai*	- - -	conj
ἐστὲ εἰμί	you are all *e·ste*	PRES ACT IND 2ND PL	verb
ἐν ἐν	in/by/with *en*	- - -	prep
αὐτῷ αὐτός	him *au·tō*	DAT SG MASC	personal pron
πεπληρωμένοι πληρόω	(those) having been filled/fulfilled *pe·plē·rō·me·noi*	PERF PASS PTCP NOM PL MASC	verb

Various translations have been offered for **πεπληρωμένοι** ("having been filled/fulfilled") here in 10a: "filled in him" (ESV, NET), "complete in him" (KJV), "brought to fullness" (NIV) or "fullness in him" (NRSV). Since Paul uses **πλήρωμα** ("fullness") to describe "the deity" (**θεότητος**) in v. 9, it seems evident that Paul is making a comparison of the "fullness" of God ("the deity") in the body of Christ and the "fullness" of the believer in the body of Christ. More importantly, what Paul is indicating is a spiritual unity between God himself and the believer, a participation or union of the believer completely with and within God himself. (See 2 Pet 1:4.)

10b	ὅς ἐστιν ἡ κεφαλὴ πάσης ἀρχῆς καὶ ἐξουσίας,		
	who is the head over every ruler and authority.		
ὅς ὅς	who/which *hos*	NOM SG MASC	relative pron
ἐστιν εἰμί	(he) is *e·stin*	PRES ACT IND 3RD SG	verb
ἡ ὁ	the *hē*	NOM SG FEM	article
κεφαλὴ κεφαλή	head *ke·pha·lē*	NOM SG FEM	noun
πάσης πᾶς	of all/each/every *pa·sēs*	GEN SG FEM	adj
ἀρχῆς ἀρχή	of beginning/ruler *ar·chēs*	GEN SG FEM	noun
καὶ καί	and *kai*	---	conj
ἐξουσίας ἐξουσία	of authority *e·xou·si·as*	GEN SG FEM	noun

11a

ἐν ᾧ καὶ περιετμήθητε

en hō kai perietmēthēte

In him you also were circumcised

11b

περιτομῇ ἀχειροποιήτῳ

peritomē acheiropoiētō

ἐν τῇ ἀπεκδύσει τοῦ σώματος τῆς σαρκός,

en tē apekdysei tou sōmatos tēs sarkos,

**with a circumcision made without hands
by the removal of the body of flesh**

11c

ἐν τῇ περιτομῇ τοῦ χριστοῦ,

en tē peritomē tou christou,

in the circumcision of Christ,

12a

συνταφέντες αὐτῷ ἐν τῷ βαπτίσματι,

syntaphentes autō en tō baptismati,

having been buried together with him in baptism,

12b

ἐν ᾧ καὶ συνηγέρθητε

en hō kai synēgerthēte

in which you were also raised with him

12c

διὰ τῆς πίστεως τῆς ἐνεργείας τοῦ θεοῦ

dia tēs pisteōs tēs energeias tou theou

through faith in the power of God,

12d

τοῦ ἐγείραντος αὐτὸν ἐκ νεκρῶν·

tou egeirantos auton ek nekrōn;

who raised him from the dead.

ἐν ᾧ καὶ περιετμήθητε

In him you also were circumcised

ἐν	in/by/with	---	prep
ἐν	*en*		
ᾧ	to whom/which	DAT SG MASC	relative
ὅς	*hō*		pron
καὶ	and/also/even	---	conj
καί	*kai*		
περιετμήθητε	you (all) were circumcised	AOR PASS IND	verb
περιτέμνω	*pe·ri·e·__tmē__·thē·te*	2ND PL	

περιτομῇ ἀχειροποιήτῳ
ἐν τῇ ἀπεκδύσει τοῦ σώματος τῆς σαρκός,

with a circumcision made without hands
by the removal of the body of flesh

περιτομῇ	to circumcision	DAT SG FEM	noun
περιτομή	*pe·ri·to·__mē__*		
ἀχειροποιήτῳ	made without hands	DAT SG FEM	adj
ἀχειροποίητος	*a·chei·ro·poi·__ē__·tō*		
ἐν	in/by/with	---	prep
ἐν	*en*		
τῇ	the	DAT SG FEM	article
ὁ	*tē*		
ἀπεκδύσει	removal	DAT SG FEM	noun
ἀπέκδυσις	*ap·ek·__dy__·sei*		
τοῦ	of the	GEN SG NEUT	article
ὁ	*tou*		
σώματος	(of) body	GEN SG NEUT	noun
σῶμα	*sō·ma·tos*		
τῆς	of the	GEN SG FEM	article
ὁ	*tēs*		
σαρκός	(of) flesh	GEN SG FEM	noun
σάρξ	*sar·__kos__*		

This verse is about a believer's identification as one who is in Christ. Paul is not suggesting that believers in Christ ought to be physically circumcised, hence "a circumcision made without hands." He is saying, rather, that the sign that believers are truly in Christ is the fact that they have been spiritually circumcised.

We can understand this phrase, "body of the flesh," in two primary ways. It could be that Paul departs from the way he has used the term "flesh" so far in Colossians (1:22, 24; 2:1, 5) and instead uses it to suggest the "fleshly nature" (that is, the body that has been corrupted by the sinful flesh), which is more common throughout his epistles (hence the NIV translation here: "your whole self ruled by the flesh"). Whereas the Colossian Christians were formerly identified by their fleshly nature (i.e., evil nature and deeds; 1:21), they are now *in Christ*, identified by their spiritual circumcision. It may also be that Paul is referring to the physical flesh, the circumcision of which was the Jewish induction rite into the people of God. If so, Paul is stating that a spiritual circumcision of the physical flesh is now the induction rite into the family of God (see Rom 2:7). Both are realities of union with Christ for Paul, and therefore both can be options theologically. Because Paul does not typically describe physical circumcision (even if in spiritual terms) with the language of both "body" (σῶμα) and "flesh" (σάρξ), it seems more likely that he has "sinful flesh" in mind (so NIV; Rom 8:13). This all the more, since Paul will return to these terms in 2:13 to refer to spiritual life and death.

11c	ἐν τῇ περιτομῇ τοῦ χριστοῦ,		
	in the circumcision of Christ,		
ἐν ἐν	in/by/with *en*	---	prep
τῇ ὁ	the *tē*	DAT SG FEM	article
περιτομῇ περιτομή	circumcision *pe·ri·to·mē*	DAT SG FEM	noun
τοῦ ὁ	of the *tou*	GEN SG MASC	article
χριστοῦ Χριστός	(of) Christ *chri·stou*	GEN SG MASC	noun

The use of the genitive ("of Christ") here raises questions: Is it a subjective genitive (a spiritual circumcision performed by Christ), an objective genitive (a physical circumcision done to Christ), or something less specific? The key question is whether Paul is even referring to traditional Jewish circumcision. The answers to these questions are hinted at in v. 12.

συνταφέντες αὐτῷ ἐν τῷ βαπτίσματι,			
having been buried together with him in baptism,			
συνταφέντες συνθάπτω	(those) having been buried together *syn·ta·phen·tes*	AOR PASS PTCP NOM PL MASC	verb
αὐτῷ αὐτός	with him *au·tō*	DAT SG MASC	personal pron
ἐν ἐν	in *en*	---	prep
τῷ ὁ	the *tō*	DAT SG NEUT	article
βαπτίσματι βάπτισμα	baptism *ba·ptis·ma·ti*	DAT SG NEUT	noun

Paul switches metaphors here and uses baptism as a metaphor for describing the Colossian Christians' new identity *in Christ*. What we see is that, for Paul, spiritual circumcision is the same as baptism into Christ. Circumcision of the "flesh" results in the same spiritual identity as baptism into Christ: union with Christ. To be circumcised *in* Christ and *by* Christ is to be baptized into Christ. Here he describes a believer's co-burial (which implies co-death) with Christ in baptism. (See also Gal 5:24 where Paul describes the same baptismal realities of co-crucifixion of the flesh.)

ἐν ᾧ καὶ συνηγέρθητε			
in which you were also raised with him			
ἐν ἐν	in/by/with *en*	---	prep
ᾧ ὅς	which *hō*	DAT SG NEUT	relative pron
καὶ καί	also *kai*	---	conj
συνηγέρθητε συνεγείρω	you (all) were raised together *syn·ē·ger·thē·te*	AOR PASS IND 2ND PL	verb

Here Paul says those who have been co-buried in baptism with Christ are also co-raised with Christ in baptism. Connecting 2:11 to 2:12, the circumcision of the "body of flesh" is the burial of the "body of flesh" and the resurrection life in Christ. See also Rom 6:3–4 and Gal 3:27. In both metaphors, the identity of the believer as one who is in Christ, and therefore in the family of God, is in focus.

12c	**διὰ τῆς πίστεως τῆς ἐνεργείας τοῦ θεοῦ**		
	through faith in the power of God		
διὰ διά	through *di·a*	---	prep
τῆς ὁ	the *tēs*	GEN SG FEM	article
πίστεως πίστις	faith *pi·ste·ōs*	GEN SG FEM	noun
τῆς ὁ	of the *tēs*	GEN SG FEM	article
ἐνεργείας ἐνέργεια	(of) power *en·er·gei·as*	GEN SG FEM	noun
τοῦ ὁ	of the *tou*	GEN SG MASC	article
θεοῦ θεός	(of) God *the·ou*	GEN SG MASC	noun

12d	**τοῦ ἐγείραντος αὐτὸν ἐκ νεκρῶν·**		
	who raised him from the dead.		
τοῦ ὁ	of the *tou*	GEN SG MASC	article
ἐγείραντος ἐγείρω	(one) having raised *e·gei·ran·tos*	AOR ACT PTCP GEN SG MASC	verb
αὐτὸν αὐτός	him *au·ton*	ACC SG MASC	personal pron
ἐκ ἐκ	from *ek*	---	prep
νεκρῶν νεκρός	dead (ones) *ne·krōn*	GEN PL MASC	adj

13a
καὶ ὑμᾶς νεκροὺς ὄντας τοῖς παραπτώμασιν
kai hymas nekrous ontas tois paraptōmasin

And you, who were all dead in your trespasses

13b
καὶ τῇ ἀκροβυστίᾳ τῆς σαρκὸς ὑμῶν,
kai tē akrobystia tēs sarkos hymōn,

and in the uncircumcision of your flesh,

13c
συνεζωοποίησεν ὑμᾶς σὺν αὐτῷ·
synezōopoiēsen hymas syn autō;

he made you alive together with him.

13d
χαρισάμενος ἡμῖν πάντα τὰ παραπτώματα,
charisamenos hēmin panta ta paraptōmata,

Having forgiven us all our trespasses,

14a
ἐξαλείψας τὸ καθ᾽ ἡμῶν χειρόγραφον τοῖς δόγμασιν
exaleipsas to kath' hēmōn cheirographon tois dogmasin

he erased the record of our debt,
which stood against us with its decrees,

14b
ὃ ἦν ὑπεναντίον ἡμῖν,
ho ēn hypenantion hēmin,

which condemned us;

14c
καὶ αὐτὸ ἦρκεν ἐκ τοῦ μέσου
kai auto ērken ek tou mesou

he has set this aside,

14d
προσηλώσας αὐτὸ τῷ σταυρῷ·
prosēlōsas auto tō staurō;

having nailed it to the cross.

15a ἀπεκδυσάμενος τὰς ἀρχὰς καὶ τὰς ἐξουσίας

apekdysamenos tas archas kai tas exousias

Having disarmed the rulers and authorities,

15b ἐδειγμάτισεν ἐν παρρησίᾳ

edeigmatisen en parrhēsia

he put them to public shame,

15c θριαμβεύσας αὐτοὺς ἐν αὐτῷ.

thriambeusas autous en autō.

having triumphed over them by the cross.

13a	**καὶ ὑμᾶς νεκροὺς ὄντας τοῖς παραπτώμασιν**		
	And you, who were all dead in your trespasses		
καὶ καί	and *kai*	---	conj
ὑμᾶς σύ	you (all) *hy·mas*	2ND ACC PL	personal pron
νεκροὺς νεκρός	dead (ones) *ne·krous*	ACC PL MASC	adj
ὄντας εἰμί	being *on·tas*	PRES ACT PTCP ACC PL MASC	verb
τοῖς ὁ	in the *tois*	DAT PL NEUT	article
παραπτώμασιν παράπτωμα	trespasses *pa·ra·ptō·ma·sin*	DAT PL NEUT	noun

13b	**καὶ τῇ ἀκροβυστίᾳ τῆς σαρκὸς ὑμῶν,**		
	and in the uncircumcision of your flesh,		
καὶ καί	and *kai*	---	conj

τῇ ὁ	in the *tē*	DAT SG FEM	article
ἀκροβυστίᾳ ἀκροβυστία	uncircumcision *a·kro·by·sti·a*	DAT SG FEM	noun
τῆς ὁ	of the *tēs*	GEN SG FEM	article
σαρκὸς σάρξ	(of) flesh *sar·kos*	GEN SG FEM	noun
ὑμῶν σύ	of you (all)/your *hy·mōn*	2ND GEN PL	personal pron

Paul returns to the language of 2:11, now clearly in spiritual terms of death and life.

13c	**συνεζωοποίησεν ὑμᾶς σὺν αὐτῷ·**		
	he made you alive together with him.		
συνεζωοποίησεν συζωοποιέω	he made alive together *syn·e·zō·o·poi·ē·sen*	AOR ACT IND 3RD SG	verb
ὑμᾶς σύ	you (all) *hy·mas*	2ND ACC PL	personal pron
σὺν σύν	with *syn*	---	prep
αὐτῷ αὐτός	him *au·tō*	DAT SG MASC	personal pron

Here is Paul's point: they were dead and are now alive. Whether through the analogy of circumcision or baptism, what Paul is getting at is that they formerly existed in a spiritual realm in which they were as good as dead, and then God rescued them from that realm and brought them into the realm of the Son he loves (1:13), where they are made alive in him. Essentially, what Paul is describing is their salvation, their rescue out of darkness and into light, the result of which is life itself in Christ.

13d	**χαρισάμενος ἡμῖν πάντα τὰ παραπτώματα,**		
	Having forgiven us all our trespasses,		
χαρισάμενος χαρίζομαι	having forgiven *cha·ri·sa·me·nos*	AOR MID PTCP NOM SG MASC	verb
ἡμῖν ἐγώ	(for) us *hē·min*	1ST DAT PL	personal pron

πάντα	all	ACC PL NEUT	adj
πᾶς	*pan·ta*		
τὰ	the	ACC PL NEUT	article
ὁ	*ta*		
παραπτώματα	trespasses	ACC PL NEUT	noun
παράπτωμα	*pa·ra·ptō·ma·ta*		

ἐξαλείψας τὸ καθ' ἡμῶν χειρόγραφον τοῖς δόγμασιν

having erased the record of our debt,
which stood against us with its decrees,

ἐξαλείψας	having erased	AOR ACT PTCP	verb
ἐξαλείφω	*ex·a·lei·psas*	NOM SG MASC	
τὸ	the	ACC SG NEUT	article
ὁ	*to*		
καθ'	against	---	prep
κατά	*kath'*		
ἡμῶν	us	1ST GEN PL	personal
ἐγώ	*hē·mōn*		pron
χειρόγραφον	record of debt	ACC SG NEUT	noun
χειρόγραφον	*chei·ro·gra·phon*		
τοῖς	with the	DAT PL NEUT	article
ὁ	*tois*		
δόγμασιν	decrees	DAT PL NEUT	noun
δόγμα	*do·gma·sin*		

Paul described forgiveness in 1:14 as part of the redemption process. Here he expands the idea as a debt to be paid, similar to the idea described in Matthew's account of the Sermon on the Mount: "Forgive us our debts as we forgive our debtors" (Matt 6:12).

ὃ ἦν ὑπεναντίον ἡμῖν,

which condemned us;

ὃ	which	NOM SG NEUT	relative
ὅς	*ho*		pron
ἦν	(it) was	IMPF ACT IND	verb
εἰμί	*ēn*	3RD SG	
ὑπεναντίον	hostile	NOM SG NEUT	adj
ὑπεναντίος	*hyp·e·nan·ti·on*		

ἡμῖν	to us	1ST DAT PL	personal
ἐγώ	hē·min		pron

14c	**καὶ αὐτὸ ἦρκεν ἐκ τοῦ μέσου**		
	he has set this aside,		

καὶ	and	---	conj
καί	*kai*		
αὐτὸ	he	ACC SG NEUT	personal
αὐτός	*au·to*		pron
ἦρκεν	(he) has taken	PERF ACT IND	verb
αἴρω	*ēr·ken*	3RD SG	
ἐκ	from	---	prep
ἐκ	*ek*		
τοῦ	the	GEN SG NEUT	article
ὁ	*tou*		
μέσου	middle	GEN SG NEUT	adj
μέσος	*me·sou*		

Here is a good example of how a robust literal translation is not helpful to the modern reader. The prepositional phrase, **ἐκ τοῦ μέσου**, literally translates to "from the middle," but can also be translated as "from (our) midst" or "out of the way."

14d	**προσηλώσας αὐτὸ τῷ σταυρῷ·**		
	having nailed it to the cross.		

προσηλώσας	(he) having nailed to	AOR ACT PTCP	verb
προσηλόω	*pros·ē·lō·sas*	NOM SG MASC	
αὐτὸ	it	ACC SG NEUT	personal
αὐτός	*au·to*		pron
τῷ	to the	DAT SG MASC	article
ὁ	*tō*		
σταυρῷ	cross	DAT SG MASC	noun
σταυρός	*stau·rō*		

That guilty verdict, the condemnation, is dealt with justly on the cross.

ἀπεκδυσάμενος τὰς ἀρχὰς καὶ τὰς ἐξουσίας
Having disarmed the rulers and authorities,

ἀπεκδυσάμενος	having disarmed	AOR MID PTCP	verb
ἀπεκδύομαι	*ap·ek·dy·sa·me·nos*	NOM SG MASC	
τὰς	the	ACC PL FEM	article
ὁ	*tas*		
ἀρχὰς	rulers	ACC PL FEM	noun
ἀρχή	*ar·chas*		
καὶ	and	---	conj
καί	*kai*		
τὰς	the	ACC PL FEM	article
ὁ	*tas*		
ἐξουσίας	authorities	ACC PL FEM	noun
ἐξουσία	*e·xou·si·as*		

Individual forgiveness of sins is a monumental result of the death of Christ on the cross. But it is not the only result. The cosmic significance of Christ's death on the cross is his defeat of evil powers and authorities, those malevolent rulers of the kingdom of darkness. The cosmic war that has raged since humans first abandoned the glory of God and replaced it with their own glory (Rom 1:21–23) has now finally pivoted toward its final battle. *On the cross* he disarmed them, stopping them in their tracks, guaranteeing God's final battle with evil will be won.

15b

ἐδειγμάτισεν ἐν παρρησίᾳ
he put them to public shame,

ἐδειγμάτισεν	he exposed	AOR ACT IND	verb
δειγματίζω	*e·deig·ma·ti·sen*	3RD SG	
ἐν	in	---	prep
ἐν	*en*		
παρρησίᾳ	openness	DAT SG FEM	noun
παρρησία	*par·rhē·si·a*		

15c

θριαμβεύσας αὐτοὺς ἐν αὐτῷ.
having triumphed over them by the cross.

θριαμβεύσας	having triumphed over	AOR ACT PTCP	verb
θριαμβεύω	*thri·am·beu·sas*	NOM SG MASC	

αὐτούς	them	ACC PL MASC	personal
αὐτός	*au·tous*		pron
ἐν	by	---	prep
ἐν	*en*		
αὐτῷ	it/him	DAT SG MASC	personal
αὐτός	*au·tō*		pron

The antecedent of the prepositional phrase **ἐν αὐτῷ** could be either Christ (so ESV, NASB, RSV) or the cross (so NKJV, KJV, NET, NIV, NRSV). Either way, what is notable here is that it is not through the resurrection that Christ defeated evil powers, but through his death on the cross. Herein is the foundational, paradoxical gospel truth: redemptive power is demonstrated first and foremost in humility, sacrifice, and suffering—a cruciform life.

From Text to Sermon

 Big Idea. Your old self has died, and you have risen to a new life in Christ. (Or, put another way, you are no longer the person you used to be.)

 Bridge to Theology. Two highly significant theological points are made in this short section.

(1) What Paul is describing with these two metaphors of circumcision and baptism is the theological concept of salvation, based on the Old Testament exodus narrative where God rescues his people from their slavery to a foreign nation. In Col 1:13 Paul says that God "rescued" us from the "dominion of darkness" in which we participated as his "enemies" (1:21) and where we practiced and found our identity in the ways of the rulers (2:15) of that dominion (3:7). Through the cross, Jesus defeated these rulers (2:15) and launched God's great rescue campaign. Through faith in Christ, we are rescued from that dominion of darkness and brought into the kingdom of the Son (1:13). We no longer give our allegiance to the rulers of the kingdom of darkness but give our allegiance to Christ (see also Rom 6:17–18). We are no longer identified by our participation in that kingdom but are now identified by Christ. We have been baptized *into* him and raised to new life *in* him. Therefore, what is true of him is true of us. This is a foundational theological point that ought to provide the basis of every believer's identity and hope. (See the discussion on participation in Christ in the "Author's Introduction" at the start of this volume.)

(2) Christ's death on the cross brought about two major changes to the history of humanity: the forgiveness of sins (2:14) and the defeat of evil (2:15). Within Paul's apocalyptic framework, Christ dealt the first death blow to evil rulers on the cross (see 1 Cor 2:8). In the divine mystery of God, the death of the Son launched the defeat of evil itself. Christ's resurrection from the dead, then, followed by his appearances (1 Cor 15:5–8), is the visible demonstration that God has, in fact, defeated death and that Jesus is the Son of God in power (Rom 1:4), the true lord of the cosmos. The gospel we proclaim to the world, therefore, must have both elements: forgiveness of sins and the defeat of evil. If it does not, then it is not the full gospel and likely will have little staying power. It is for this reason that the cosmic gospel ought to have implications for all aspects of reality (see 1:15–23 discussions).

Illustrations/Applications. The power of God was demonstrated through the cross, the ultimate form of sacrifice. It is important for all believers to ask the question, "What does it look like to participate in the redemptive work of God in the world?" It looks like participation in the death, burial, and resurrection of Christ—living out our identity in Christ. At times it looks like celebrating or creating beauty, sharing love, offering praise, cherishing friendships, and recognizing the good in the world. At other times it looks like struggling for justice, reconciliation, or redemption in the midst of fractured systems, hearts, relationships, and communities.

Here we are, again, asking the question: What does the gospel of Christ have to do with things like politics, finances, or the environment? Perhaps more pointedly, what does the gospel of Christ have to say to things like systematic oppression, war, famine, modern-day slavery, sex trafficking, our treatment of orphans or foreigners, racism, sexism, domestic abuse, child pornography (and *so much more*)? And what is our role in the redemption/elimination of these things from the good, created world? If we truly live out our identities as full participants in the life of Christ, then our lives will reflect Christ's work on the cross and his resurrection from the grave. The gospel we proclaim has just as much to do with the establishment of the kingdom of God on earth as it does with our individual need for justification or forgiveness. God is working to bring this redemption through his people (cf. 2 Cor 5:16–6:2). Here's an excellent opportunity to challenge your congregation to proclaim the gospel of Christ in ways that go beyond the "Four Spiritual Laws" or a "Romans Road" description or a "Jesus Bridge" illustration. If we miss this point, we miss Colossians. And we miss one of the fundamental reasons God became incarnate in this present evil age (Gal 1:4).

RULED ONLY BY CHRIST

In this section, Paul begins to challenge the church in Colossae to live out their new identity in Christ. It is precisely because of their identity in Christ that they ought not to obey the regulations of the human-made religion that is sweeping through the church there. Their old selves have died with Christ (2:20) and their new selves have been raised with/in Christ (3:1). Therefore, as those hidden with Christ in God (3:3), they have freedom to live for Christ and under the rule of Christ.

16a
Μὴ οὖν τις ὑμᾶς κρινέτω

Mē oun tis hymas krinetō

Therefore, do not let anyone judge you

16b
ἐν βρώσει καὶ ἐν πόσει

en brōsei kai en posei

ἢ ἐν μέρει ἑορτῆς ἢ νεομηνίας ἢ σαββάτων,

ē en merei heortēs ē neomēnias ē sabbatōn,

in matters of what you eat or drink,
or in your observance of festivals, new moons, or sabbaths,

17a
ἅ ἐστιν σκιὰ τῶν μελλόντων,

ha estin skia tōn mellontōn,

which are a shadow of the things about to come;

17b
τὸ δὲ σῶμα τοῦ χριστοῦ.

to de sōma tou christou.

but the present reality is the body of Christ.

18a
μηδεὶς ὑμᾶς καταβραβευέτω

mēdeis hymas katabrabeuetō

Do not let anyone disqualify you,

18b
θέλων ἐν ταπεινοφροσύνῃ

thelōn en tapeinophrosynē

insisting on false humility

18c
καὶ θρησκείᾳ τῶν ἀγγέλων,

kai thrēskeia tōn angelōn,

and in the worship of angels,

18d

ἃ ἑόρακεν ἐμβατεύων,

ha heoraken embateuōn,

dwelling on what he has seen,

18e

εἰκῇ φυσιούμενος ὑπὸ τοῦ νοὸς τῆς σαρκὸς αὐτοῦ,

eikē physioumenos hypo tou noos tēs sarkos autou,

being vainly puffed up in his fleshly mind.

19a

καὶ οὐ κρατῶν τὴν κεφαλήν,

kai ou kratōn tēn kephalēn,

He has lost his connection with the head,

19b

ἐξ οὗ πᾶν τὸ σῶμα

ex hou pan to sōma

from whom the whole body,

19c

διὰ τῶν ἁφῶν καὶ συνδέσμων

dia tōn haphōn kai syndesmōn

ἐπιχορηγούμενον καὶ συνβιβαζόμενον

epichorēgoumenon kai synbibazomenon

which is nourished and held together by its joints and ligaments,

19d

αὔξει τὴν αὔξησιν τοῦ θεοῦ.

auxei tēn auxēsin tou theou.

grows as God causes it to grow.

16a	**Μὴ οὖν τις ὑμᾶς κρινέτω**		
	Therefore, do not let anyone judge you		
Μὴ μή	not *Mē*	---	particle
οὖν οὖν	therefore *oun*	---	conj

τις	anyone	NOM SG MASC	indef
τίς	tis		pron
ὑμᾶς	you (all)	2ND ACC PL	personal
σύ	hy·**mas**		pron
κρινέτω	let (him) judge	PRES ACT IMPV	verb
κρίνω	kri·**ne**·tō	3RD SG	

The **οὖν** ("therefore") at the start of this verse marks a transition. The previous sections—Christ's supremacy and the redemption it brings (1:15–23), Paul's comments on his ministry (1:24–2:7), and the realities of the church's new identity in Christ (2:8–15)—are the facts on the ground and thus use the indicative mood. They were concerned with establishing what is true. Beginning in Col 2:16, Paul switches to the imperative ("Therefore, go and do . . .") and challenges the Colossians to go and live *on the basis of those truths.*

16b	ἐν βρώσει καὶ ἐν πόσει ἢ ἐν μέρει ἑορτῆς ἢ νεομηνίας ἢ σαββάτων,		
	in matters of what you eat or drink, or in your observance of festivals, new moons, or sabbaths,		

ἐν	in	---	prep
ἐν	en		
βρώσει	food	DAT SG FEM	noun
βρῶσις	**brō**·sei		
καὶ	and	---	conj
καί	**kai**		
ἐν	in	---	prep
ἐν	en		
πόσει	drink	DAT SG FEM	noun
πόσις	**po**·sei		
ἤ	or	---	particle
ἤ	ē		
ἐν	in	---	prep
ἐν	en		
μέρει	regard	DAT SG NEUT	noun
μέρος	**me**·rei		
ἑορτῆς	of festival	GEN SG FEM	noun
ἑορτή	he·or·**tēs**		
ἤ	or	---	particle
ἤ	ē		
νεομηνίας	of new moon	GEN SG FEM	noun
νουμηνία	ne·o·mē·**ni**·as		

ἤ	or	---	particle
ἤ	*ē*		
σαββάτων	of sabbaths	GEN PL NEUT	noun
σάββατον	*sab·ba·tōn*		

<table>
<tr><td>17a</td><td colspan="3" align="center">ἅ ἐστιν σκιὰ τῶν μελλόντων,</td></tr>
</table>

which are a shadow of the things about to come;

ἅ	which (ones)	NOM PL NEUT	relative
ὅς	*ha*		pron
ἐστιν	(it) is	PRES ACT IND	verb
εἰμί	*e·stin*	3RD SG	
σκιὰ	shadow	NOM SG FEM	noun
σκιά	*ski·a*		
τῶν	of the	GEN PL NEUT	article
ὁ	*tōn*		
μελλόντων	(of) things about to be	PRES ACT PTCP	verb
μέλλω	*mel·lon·tōn*	GEN PL NEUT	

<table>
<tr><td>17b</td><td colspan="3" align="center">τὸ δὲ σῶμα τοῦ χριστοῦ.</td></tr>
</table>

but the present reality is the body of Christ.

τὸ	the	NOM SG NEUT	article
ὁ	*to*		
δὲ	but	---	conj
δέ	*de*		
σῶμα	body	NOM SG NEUT	noun
σῶμα	*sō·ma*		
τοῦ	of the	GEN SG MASC	article
ὁ	*tou*		
χριστοῦ	(of) Christ	GEN SG MASC	noun
Χριστός	*chri·stou*		

This clause contains a subject without a verb. The subject, **τὸ . . . σῶμα**, indicates something more like "substance" or "reality" than it does "body," since it stands in contrast with **σκιὰ** ("shadow") in 17a. The contrast drawn here is between the shadow, the thing that is passing (e.g., the Torah, food laws, the sacrificial system, etc.), or that always only pointed toward the real thing to come, and the present reality, namely the fullness of life in Christ.

μηδεὶς ὑμᾶς καταβραβευέτω

Do not let anyone disqualify you,

μηδεὶς μηδείς	no one *mē·**deis***	NOM SG MASC	adj
ὑμᾶς σύ	you (all) *hy·**mas***	2ND ACC PL	personal pron
καταβραβευέτω καταβραβεύω	let (him) judge *ka·ta·bra·beu·e·tō*	PRES ACT IMPV 3RD SG	verb

θέλων ἐν ταπεινοφροσύνῃ

insisting on false humility

θέλων θέλω	desiring *the·lōn*	PRES ACT PTCP NOM SG MASC	verb
ἐν ἐν	in *en*	---	prep
ταπεινοφροσύνῃ ταπεινοφροσύνη	humility *ta·pei·no·phro·sy·nē*	DAT SG FEM	noun

Paul's use of **ταπεινοφροσύνη** here implies something other than a virtuous humility. In this case, he likely refers to the false teachers' false humility demonstrated in their ascetic practices related especially to food practices (2:16). This is especially the case given that the false teachers are also said to be "vainly puffed up" (**εἰκῇ φυσιούμενος**) at the end of this v. 18.

καὶ θρησκείᾳ τῶν ἀγγέλων,

and in the worship of angels,

καὶ καί	and *kai*	---	conj
θρησκείᾳ θρησκεία	religion *thrē·skei·a*	DAT SG FEM	noun
τῶν ὁ	of the *tōn*	GEN PL MASC	article
ἀγγέλων ἄγγελος	(of) angels *an·ge·lōn*	GEN PL MASC	noun

18d

ἃ ἑόρακεν ἐμβατεύων,			
dwelling on what he has seen,			
ἃ	which (things)	ACC PL NEUT	relative
ὅς	*ha*		pron
ἑόρακεν	he has seen	PERF ACT IND	verb
ὁράω	*he·o·ra·ken*	3RD SG	
ἐμβατεύων	entering	PRES ACT PTCP	verb
ἐμβατεύω	*em·ba·teu·ōn*	NOM SG MASC	

18e

εἰκῇ φυσιούμενος ὑπὸ τοῦ νοὸς τῆς σαρκὸς αὐτοῦ,			
being vainly puffed up in his fleshly mind.			
εἰκῇ	vainly	---	adv
εἰκῇ	*ei·kē*		
φυσιούμενος	being puffed up	PRES PASS PTCP	verb
φυσιόω	*phy·si·ou·me·nos*	NOM SG MASC	
ὑπὸ	by	---	prep
ὑπό	*hy·po*		
τοῦ	the	GEN SG MASC	article
ὁ	*tou*		
νοὸς	understanding	GEN SG MASC	noun
νοῦς	*no·os*		
τῆς	of the	GEN SG FEM	article
ὁ	*tēs*		
σαρκὸς	(of) flesh	GEN SG FEM	noun
σάρξ	*sar·kos*		
αὐτοῦ	of him/his	GEN SG MASC	personal
αὐτός	*au·tou*		pron

Here Paul clearly uses **σάρξ** ("flesh") not in reference to the physical skin or body but as a negative connotation of a sinful reality: his mind is ruled by the Flesh (see 2:11).

19a

καὶ οὐ κρατῶν τὴν κεφαλήν,			
He has lost his connection with the head,			
καὶ	and	---	conj
καί	*kai*		
οὐ	not	---	particle
οὐ	*ou*		

κρατῶν	(one) holding fast	PRES ACT PTCP	verb
κρατέω	kra·tōn	NOM SG MASC	
τὴν	the	ACC SG FEM	article
ὁ	tēn		
κεφαλήν	head	ACC SG FEM	noun
κεφαλή	ke·pha·lēn		

Readers should note that 2:19a is a subordinate clause to 2:18a, in what is a typically long sentence for Colossians. For the sake of a more accessible translation, I have chosen to start a new sentence at 2:19a.

19b	**ἐξ οὗ πᾶν τὸ σῶμα**		
	from whom the whole body,		
ἐξ	from	---	prep
ἐκ	ex		
οὗ	of which	GEN SG MASC	relative
ὅς	hou		pron
πᾶν	all	NOM SG NEUT	adj
πᾶς	pan		
τὸ	the	NOM SG NEUT	article
ὁ	to		
σῶμα	body	NOM SG NEUT	noun
σῶμα	sō·ma		

19c	**διὰ τῶν ἀφῶν καὶ συνδέσμων** **ἐπιχορηγούμενον καὶ συνβιβαζόμενον**		
	which is nourished and held together by its joints and ligaments,		
διὰ	through	---	prep
διά	di·a		
τῶν	the	GEN PL FEM	article
ὁ	tōn		
ἀφῶν	joints	GEN PL FEM	noun
ἀφή	ha·phōn		
καὶ	and	---	conj
καί	kai		
συνδέσμων	ligaments	GEN PL MASC	noun
σύνδεσμος	syn·de·smōn		
ἐπιχορηγούμενον	being supplied	PRES PASS PTCP	verb
ἐπιχορηγέω	e·pi·cho·rē·gou·me·non	NOM SG NEUT	

καὶ καί	and *kai*	---	conj
συνβιβαζόμενον συμβιβάζω	being brought together *syn·bi·ba·zo·me·non*	PRES PASS PTCP NOM SG NEUT	verb

19d	**αὔξει τὴν αὔξησιν τοῦ θεοῦ.**
	grows as God causes it to grow.

αὔξει αὐξάνω	(it) grows *au·xei*	PRES ACT IND 3RD SG 3RD SG	verb
τὴν ὁ	the *tēn*	ACC SG FEM	article
αὔξησιν αὔξησις	growth *au·xē·sin*	ACC SG FEM	noun
τοῦ ὁ	of the *tou*	GEN SG MASC	article
θεοῦ θεός	(of) God *the·ou*	GEN SG MASC	noun

Paul challenges the Colossian believers in this verse not to be persuaded by the false teacher who is "puffed up" and has "lost his connection with the head" (v. 19), Christ. The false teacher, therefore, is no longer connected to the growing body of Christ, the church itself.

20a   Εἰ ἀπεθάνετε σὺν Χριστῷ ἀπὸ τῶν στοιχείων τοῦ κόσμου,
       Ei apethanete syn Christō apo tōn stoicheiōn tou kosmou,

Since you died with Christ to the elemental spirits of the world,

20b   τί ὡς ζῶντες ἐν κόσμῳ δογματίζεσθε,
       ti hōs zōntes en kosmō dogmatizesthe,

why do you still live as those who belong to the world—

21a   Μὴ ἅψῃ
               Mē hapsē

"Do not handle,

21b   μηδὲ γεύσῃ
               mēde geusē

do not taste,

21c   μηδὲ θίγῃς,
               mēde thigēs,

do not touch"—

22a   ἅ ἐστιν πάντα εἰς φθορὰν τῇ ἀποχρήσει,
       ha estin panta eis phthoran tē apochrēsei,

(all of which are perishing with use)—

22b   κατὰ τὰ ἐντάλματα καὶ διδασκαλίας τῶν ἀνθρώπων;
       kata ta entalmata kai didaskalias tōn anthrōpōn;

according to the regulations and teachings of people?

23a   ἅτινά ἐστιν λόγον μὲν ἔχοντα σοφίας
       hatina estin logon men echonta sophias

These regulations indeed have the appearance of wisdom—

23b   ἐν ἐθελοθρησκίᾳ
               en ethelothrēskia

in self-imposed piety,

23c

καὶ ταπεινοφροσύνῃ

kai tapeinophrosynē

and false humility

23d

[καὶ] ἀφειδίᾳ σώματος,

[kai] apheidia sōmatos,

and harmful treatment of the body,

23e

οὐκ ἐν τιμῇ τινι πρὸς πλησμονὴν τῆς σαρκός.

ouk en timē tini pros plēsmonēn tēs sarkos.

but are of no value in restraining the indulgence of the flesh.

20a	Εἰ ἀπεθάνετε σὺν Χριστῷ ἀπὸ τῶν στοιχείων τοῦ κόσμου,
	Since you died with Christ to the elemental spirits of the world,

Εἰ	if/since	---	cond
εἰ	*Ei*		
ἀπεθάνετε	you (all) died	AOR ACT IND	verb
ἀποθνήσκω	*ap·e·__tha__·ne·te*	2ND PL	
σὺν	with	---	prep
σύν	**syn**		
Χριστῷ	Christ	DAT SG MASC	noun
Χριστός	*Chri·__stō__*		
ἀπὸ	from	---	prep
ἀπό	*a·__po__*		
τῶν	the	GEN PL NEUT	article
ὁ	*tōn*		
στοιχείων	elemental spirits	GEN PL NEUT	noun
στοιχεῖον	*stoi·__chei__·ōn*		
τοῦ	of the	GEN SG MASC	article
ὁ	*tou*		
κόσμου	(of) world	GEN SG MASC	noun
κόσμος	*__ko__·smou*		

20b	**τί ὡς ζῶντες ἐν κόσμῳ δογματίζεσθε,**		
why do you still live as those who belong to the world—			

τί τίς	why? *ti*	ACC SG NEUT	interr pron
ὡς ὡς	as *hōs*	---	adv
ζῶντες ζάω	(those) living *zōn·tes*	PRES ACT PTCP NOM PL MASC	verb
ἐν ἐν	in *en*	---	prep
κόσμῳ κόσμος	world *ko·smō*	DAT SG MASC	noun
δογματίζεσθε δογματίζω	you (all) obeyed *dog·ma·ti·ze·sthe*	PRES PASS IND 2ND PL	verb

Here, again, Paul is challenging the Colossian Christians to live lives that demonstrate their true identities. They are under the lordship of Christ and not the rule of any earthly power or angelic spiritual power.

21a	**Μὴ ἅψῃ**		
"Do not handle,			

| **Μὴ**
μή | not
Mē | --- | particle |
| **ἅψῃ**
ἅπτομαι | you might handle
ha·psē | AOR MID SUBJ
2ND SG | verb |

21b	**μηδὲ γεύσῃ**		
do not taste,			

| **μηδὲ**
μηδέ | neither
mē·de | --- | conj |
| **γεύσῃ**
γεύομαι | you might taste
geu·sē | AOR MID SUBJ
2ND SG | verb |

μηδὲ θίγης,

do not touch"—

μηδὲ μηδέ	neither mē·de	---	conj
θίγης θιγγάνω	you might touch **thi**·gēs	AOR ACT SUBJ 2ND SG	verb

ἅ ἐστιν πάντα εἰς φθορὰν τῇ ἀποχρήσει,

(all of which are perishing with use)—

ἅ ὅς	which (ones) **ha**	NOM PL NEUT	relative pron
ἐστιν εἰμί	(it) is e·stin	PRES ACT IND 3RD SG	verb
πάντα πᾶς	all (things) **pan**·ta	NOM PL NEUT	adj
εἰς εἰς	into eis	---	prep
φθορὰν φθορά	decay phtho·**ran**	ACC SG FEM	noun
τῇ ὁ	to the tē	DAT SG FEM	article
ἀποχρήσει ἀπόχρησις	using up a·po·**chrĕ**·sei	DAT SG FEM	noun

κατὰ τὰ ἐντάλματα καὶ διδασκαλίας τῶν ἀνθρώπων;

according to the regulations and teachings of people?

κατὰ κατά	according to ka·**ta**	---	prep
τὰ ὁ	the **ta**	ACC PL NEUT	article
ἐντάλματα ἔνταλμα	commandments en·**tal**·ma·ta	ACC PL NEUT	noun
καὶ καί	and **kai**	---	conj
διδασκαλίας διδασκαλία	teachings di·da·ska·**li**·as	ACC PL FEM	noun
τῶν ὁ	of the **tōn**	GEN PL MASC	article

| ἀνθρώπων | (of) humanity | GEN PL MASC | noun |
| ἄνθρωπος | an·thrō·pōn | | |

<table>
<tr><td>23a</td><td colspan="3">ἅτινά ἐστιν λόγον μὲν ἔχοντα σοφίας</td></tr>
<tr><td colspan="4">These regulations indeed have the appearance of wisdom—</td></tr>
</table>

ἅτινά	such (ones)	NOM PL NEUT	relative
ὅστις	ha·ti·na		pron
ἐστιν	(it) is	PRES ACT IND	verb
εἰμί	e·stin	3RD SG	
λόγον	word	ACC SG MASC	noun
λόγος	lo·gon		
μὲν	indeed	---	particle
μέν	men		
ἔχοντα	(ones) having	PRES ACT PTCP	verb
ἔχω	e·chon·ta	NOM PL NEUT	
σοφίας	of wisdom	GEN SG FEM	noun
σοφία	so·phi·as		

<table>
<tr><td>23b</td><td colspan="3">ἐν ἐθελοθρησκίᾳ</td></tr>
<tr><td colspan="4">in self-imposed piety,</td></tr>
</table>

ἐν	in	---	prep
ἐν	en		
ἐθελοθρησκίᾳ	self-made piety	DAT SG FEM	noun
ἐθελοθρησκία	e·the·lo·thrē·ski·a		

There are several options for translating the word ἐθελοθρησκίᾳ: "self-made" or "self-imposed," "worship" or "piety" or "religion."

<table>
<tr><td>23c</td><td colspan="3">καὶ ταπεινοφροσύνῃ</td></tr>
<tr><td colspan="4">and false humility</td></tr>
</table>

καὶ	and	---	conj
καί	kai		
ταπεινοφροσύνῃ	humility	DAT SG FEM	noun
ταπεινοφροσύνη	ta·pei·no·phro·sy·nē		

Just as in 2:18, Paul is not praising the false teachers for their humility (**ταπεινοφροσύνη**). Instead, he again refers to the strict ascetic practices promoted by the false teachers, which in this case might lead to harmful treatment of the body, as he goes on to mention in the following clause.

23d	**[καὶ] ἀφειδίᾳ σώματος,**		
	and harmful treatment of the body,		
καὶ	and	---	conj
καί	*kai*		
ἀφειδίᾳ	neglect	DAT SG FEM	noun
ἀφειδία	*a·phei·di·a*		
σώματος	of body	GEN SG NEUT	noun
σῶμα	*sō·ma·tos*		

23e	**οὐκ ἐν τιμῇ τινι πρὸς πλησμονὴν τῆς σαρκός.**		
	but are of no value in restraining the indulgence of the flesh.		
οὐκ	not	---	particle
οὐ	*ouk*		
ἐν	in	---	prep
ἐν	*en*		
τιμῇ	value	DAT SG FEM	noun
τιμή	*ti·mē*		
τινι	any	DAT SG FEM	indef
τίς	*ti·ni*		pron
πρὸς	toward	---	prep
πρός	*pros*		
πλησμονὴν	indulgence	ACC SG FEM	noun
πλησμονή	*plē·smo·nēn*		
τῆς	of the	GEN SG FEM	article
ὁ	*tēs*		
σαρκός	(of) flesh	GEN SG FEM	noun
σάρξ	*sar·kos*		

This verse makes the most sense when **πρὸς** is translated as "against" rather than "for" or "toward." We see now that the "flesh" (**σάρξ**) is actually part of the realm of evil out of which the Christian has been rescued. While Paul earlier used the term **σάρξ** as a neutral reference to the physical body (1:22, 24), this reference to the "Flesh" as an evil spiritual entity is more common to Paul's epistles (e.g., Gal 5:17). The "Flesh" it-self is one of the spiritual powers that was triumphed over by Christ on the cross. The question Paul raises for the church here is why it is still being indulged, as if it were still in power, as if Christ had not already defeated it.

1a

Εἰ οὖν συνηγέρθητε τῷ χριστῷ,

Ei oun synēgerthēte tō christō,

Therefore, since you have been raised with Christ,

1b

τὰ ἄνω ζητεῖτε,

ta anō zēteite,

seek the things that are above,

1c

οὗ ὁ χριστός ἐστιν

hou ho christos estin

where Christ is,

1d

ἐν δεξιᾷ τοῦ θεοῦ καθήμενος·

en dexia tou theou kathēmenos;

seated at the right hand of God.

2a

τὰ ἄνω φρονεῖτε,

ta anō phroneite,

Set your minds on things above,

2b

μὴ τὰ ἐπὶ τῆς γῆς,

mē ta epi tēs gēs,

not on earthly things.

3a

ἀπεθάνετε γάρ,

apethanete gar,

For you have died,

3b

καὶ ἡ ζωὴ ὑμῶν κέκρυπται

kai hē zōē hymōn kekryptai

and your life is hidden

3c	σὺν τῷ χριστῷ ἐν τῷ θεῷ·

syn tō christō en tō theo;

with Christ in God.

4a	ὅταν ὁ χριστὸς φανερωθῇ, ἡ ζωὴ ὑμῶν,

hotan ho christos phanerōthē, hē zōē hymōn,

When Christ is revealed, who is your life,

4b	τότε καὶ ὑμεῖς σὺν αὐτῷ φανερωθήσεσθε ἐν δόξῃ.

tote kai hymeis syn autō phanerōthēsesthe en doxē.

then you also will be revealed with him in glory.

1a	**Εἰ οὖν συνηγέρθητε τῷ χριστῷ,**
	Therefore, since you have been raised with Christ,

Εἰ εἰ	if/since *Ei*	---	cond
οὖν οὖν	therefore *oun*	---	conj
συνηγέρθητε συνεγείρω	you (all) were raised together *syn·ē·ger·thē·te*	AOR PASS IND 2ND PL	verb
τῷ ὁ	with the *tō*	DAT SG MASC	article
χριστῷ Χριστός	Christ *chri·stō*	DAT SG MASC	noun

Notice how this clause parallels 2:20a. The focus in 2:20 is on the results of dying with Christ, whereas here the focus is on the results of being raised with Christ. Paul begins this section with what is perhaps the most important sentence in the entire letter to the Colossians. Paul uses an εἰ οὖν construction ("since therefore"). *Since* the Colossian believers have died with Christ to their old selves that were ruled over by evil powers, and since they have been raised to new life in Christ, the true lord of the cosmos, they ought *therefore* to live out that new reality, the new freedom they have in Christ. In Paul's anthropology and ecclesiology, this is the most powerful, fundamental, and eternal truth: if you were buried with Christ in baptism, then you were also raised with Christ to new life. This new life in Christ is characterized by being a new creation (2 Cor 5:17), being reconciled to God (2 Cor 5:19), being dead to sin and alive to God (Rom 6:11), being a child of God (Gal 3:26; cf. Rom 8:29), and so much more. The believer now has freedom to live for Christ and in participation with Christ. Paul's statements here on the resurrection life of believers in Christ draw to a conclusion his emphasis on this new baptismal reality of death and life in Christ, the reality on which every believer ought to build his or her life (and not on the commandments of humanity).

1b	τὰ ἄνω ζητεῖτε,		
	seek the things that are above,		
τὰ ὁ	the (things) *ta*	ACC PL NEUT	article
ἄνω ἄνω	above *a·nō*	---	adv
ζητεῖτε ζητέω	you (all) seek *zē·tei·te*	PRES ACT IMPV 2ND PL	verb

The Colossians are to "seek the things that are above." Paul challenges the Colossians to pursue the fullness of the new life in Christ, the true lord of the cosmos. Because they have been raised with Christ, they ought to live a life that demonstrates they are now ruled by and worship the creator of the heavens. The believer has been united with Christ and, therefore, his or her life ought to be characterized by the things that characterized the life of Christ. He does not go into specifics here as he will in 3:5–17; his emphasis here in 3:1–4 remains on their new identity in Christ and subjection to Christ rather than on specific actions as a believer in Christ (see 3:5–17).

1c	οὗ ὁ χριστός ἐστιν		
	where Christ is,		
οὗ οὗ	where *hou*	---	adv
ὁ ὁ	the *ho*	NOM SG MASC	article

χριστός Χριστός	Christ *chri·**stos***	NOM SG MASC	noun
ἐστιν εἰμί	(he) is *e·**stin***	PRES ACT IND 3RD SG	verb

1d	**ἐν δεξιᾷ τοῦ θεοῦ καθήμενος·**
	seated at the right hand of God.

ἐν ἐν	in *en*	---	prep
δεξιᾷ δεξιός	right (side) *de·xi·**a***	DAT SG FEM	adj
τοῦ ὁ	of the ***tou***	GEN SG MASC	article
θεοῦ θεός	(of) God *the·**ou***	GEN SG MASC	noun
καθήμενος κάθημαι	seated *ka·**thē**·me·nos*	PRES PASS PTCP NOM SG MASC	verb

In this and the previous clause, Paul is making two distinct assertions: (1) Christ is in the heavenly realms, and (2) Christ rules over the heavenly realms. Unlike the powers of evil that he defeated on the cross, he is the true lord of the cosmos.

2a	**τὰ ἄνω φρονεῖτε,**
	Set your minds on things above,

τὰ ὁ	the (things) *ta*	ACC PL NEUT	article
ἄνω ἄνω	above *a·**nō***	---	adv
φρονεῖτε φρονέω	you (all) think *phro·**nei**·te*	PRES ACT IMPV 2ND PL	verb

One of the ways in which believers "seek the things that are above" is to set their mind on those things that are clearly under the rule of Christ. One's actions are determined by one's thoughts.

μὴ τὰ ἐπὶ τῆς γῆς,			
not on earthly things.			
μὴ μή	not *mē*	---	particle
τὰ ὁ	the (things) *ta*	ACC PL NEUT	article
ἐπὶ ἐπί	on/upon *e·pi*	---	prep
τῆς ὁ	the *tēs*	GEN SG FEM	article
γῆς γῆ	earth *gēs*	GEN SG FEM	noun

These "earthly things" are those things which are under the rule of evil powers, including commands and teachings from fellow humans (so 2:16–23). Such false teachings are not rooted in Christ, ruler of the cosmos, but in humans and evil rulers who stand in opposition to the rule and reign of Christ.

3a	**ἀπεθάνετε γάρ,**		
	For you have died,		
ἀπεθάνετε ἀποθνήσκω	you (all) died *ap·e·tha·ne·te*	AOR ACT IND 2ND PL	verb
γάρ γάρ	for *gar*	---	conj

3b	**καὶ ἡ ζωὴ ὑμῶν κέκρυπται**		
	and your life is hidden		
καὶ καί	and *kai*	---	conj
ἡ ὁ	the *hē*	NOM SG FEM	article
ζωὴ ζωή	life *zŏ·ē*	NOM SG FEM	noun
ὑμῶν σύ	of you (all)/your *hy·mōn*	2ND GEN PL	personal pron
κέκρυπται κρύπτω	(it) has been hidden *ke·kryp·tai*	PERF PASS IND 3RD SG	verb

The life of the believer is no longer his or her own, and as a result of that, it has been "hidden" in something external to himself or herself.

3c	σὺν τῷ χριστῷ ἐν τῷ θεῷ·			
	with Christ in God.			
σὺν	with	---		prep
σύν	*syn*			
τῷ	the	DAT SG MASC		article
ὁ	*tō*			
χριστῷ	Christ	DAT SG MASC		noun
Χριστός	*chri·stō*			
ἐν	in	---		prep
ἐν	*en*			
τῷ	the	DAT SG MASC		article
ὁ	*tō*			
θεῷ	God	DAT SG MASC		noun
θεός	*the·ō*			

That external location in which the believer's true life is now hidden is "with Christ in God," in the heavenly realms. Paul hearkens back to Col 1:19 and especially 2:9–10. By all earthly appearances, the believer exists on earth. For Paul, though, those who have died with Christ and been raised to new life in and with Christ now find their truest existence not on earth but with Christ in the heavenly realms. And, because the fullness of God exists within Christ, believers are brought into that fullness; their identity and sheer existence is now defined by God himself in Christ. This is a foundational soteriological truth for Paul.

4a	ὅταν ὁ χριστὸς φανερωθῇ, ἡ ζωὴ ὑμῶν,			
	When Christ is revealed, who is your life,			
ὅταν	when	---		conj
ὅταν	*ho·tan*			
ὁ	the	NOM SG MASC		article
ὁ	*ho*			
χριστὸς	Christ	NOM SG MASC		noun
Χριστός	*chri·stos*			
φανερωθῇ	(he) might be revealed	AOR PASS SUBJ		verb
φανερόω	*pha·ne·rō·thē*	3RD SG		

ἡ	the	NOM SG FEM	article
ὁ	*hē*		
ζωὴ	life	NOM SG FEM	noun
ζωή	*zō·ē*		
ὑμῶν	of you (all)/your	2ND GEN PL	personal
σύ	*hy·mōn*		pron

Paul uses **φανερόω** ("to reveal") here to describe the revelation of Christ, a concept that is well within his apocalyptic framework. God has already revealed the mystery kept hidden from the ages once: the life, death, resurrection, and ascension of Jesus Christ. He will reveal him again at his parousia.

4b	**τότε καὶ ὑμεῖς σὺν αὐτῷ φανερωθήσεσθε ἐν δόξῃ.**
	then you also will be revealed with him in glory.

τότε	then	---	adv
τότε	*to·te*		
καὶ	and/also	---	conj
καί	*kai*		
ὑμεῖς	you (all)	2ND NOM PL	personal
σύ	*hy·meis*		pron
σὺν	with	---	prep
σύν	*syn*		
αὐτῷ	him	DAT SG MASC	personal
αὐτός	*au·tō*		pron
φανερωθήσεσθε	(you all) will be revealed	FUT PASS IND	verb
φανερόω	*pha·ne·rō·thē·se·sthe*	2ND PL	
ἐν	in	---	prep
ἐν	*en*		
δόξῃ	glory	DAT SG FEM	noun
δόξα	*do·xē*		

At the parousia of Christ, the lives of believers now hidden in Christ in the heavenly realms will also be revealed. This is the hope for which we live: when our true identity as participants in the kingdom of God, ruled over by the lordship of Christ, is made known to the world, and when we, too, are established in glory, perhaps the same glory that was lost in our former lives as participants in the kingdom of darkness (see Rom 3:23).

Big Idea. Do not live according to the wisdom of the world but according to the wisdom of God.

 Bridge to Theology. It's in these verses that we read about what has been named the "Colossian heresy." Worthy of remark here is the emphasis on the fact that the Colossians are not obligated to follow "regulations" that have "the appearance of wisdom" but which ultimately "are of no value in restraining the indulgence of the flesh" (2:23). They are so because they are based on "regulations and teachings of people" (2:22) instead of the "wisdom and understanding that the Spirit gives" (1:9). As with the rest of the letter, the reason why we ought not to live according to the precepts set by people is because our identity is not of the world but *in Christ*. What's true of him is true of us. Therefore, if he is at the right hand of the Father, then so are we. (Which is why Paul can write in Eph 2:6 that "God raised us up with Christ and seated us with him in the heavenly realms in Christ Jesus" [NIV].) Our lives ought to model the life of Christ because *that's who we are in our most authentic, real, true, genuine self.*

 Illustrations/Applications. Unlike the previous passages of Colossians, where Paul's focus was more on orthodoxy rather than orthopraxy, this section turns a corner with the grand "therefore" in 2:16. The possibilities for illustrations are now seemingly boundless.

You could challenge your congregants to think about their own standards for Christian piety. To what extent do church expectations of "doing devotions" in the morning or evening serve to tick a human-made box rather than a God-made box? Or to what extent is our Christian piety expressed in the music we listen to or the movies we watch? How much of these practices are cultural expectations at this moment in time rather than God's expectations for what is deemed pietistic or spiritual or wise?

To what extent is culture, rather than God, responsible for dictating what is most Christian in terms of our lifestyle? At what point is the size of a house too large? What kind of vehicle is too immodest for a Christian? Ought Christians only to eat eggs laid by chickens with the ability to roam free and eat bugs? Ought Christians only to be vegetarians? Should Christians allow their children to believe in a Tooth Fairy or an Easter Bunny or a Santa Claus (or other cultural equivalents)? Should Christians not dance or drink alcohol or smoke? Should Christian households all have a father that works outside the home and a mother that remains at home with the children? The point is that these are all cultural (that is, made by people) regulations that some, but not all, Christians deem wise and necessary for Christian/godly living. Not unlike what the Colossians experienced, we, too, need to be hyperaware of the ways in which we allow the church or the Christian culture of our day dictate for us what is the wise, pietistic, or godly way to live for Christ.

You could also turn the conversation inward to examine your own church practices regarding worship music, liturgy, Bible translations, clothing expectations, and so much more. It doesn't take long to realize how much our church culture is built on human expectations rather than God's.

VICES AND VIRTUES OF DEATH AND LIFE

The church in Colossae has found new life in Christ. They now need to live out that life, and the way to do so is to strip off, put to death, and say goodbye to the life they once knew. In this section Paul emphasizes that the believers in Colossae can't live fully in that new reality until they completely do away with their former reality. This section contains five imperatives; two are positive and three are negative. Together they describe how the believer ought to act toward their neighbor, as a result of their union with Christ. New life in Christ means new life together. For this to happen, the believers in Colossae need to "put on" the things of Christ, not only for themselves as individuals but also for the sake of the larger body.

5a   Νεκρώσατε οὖν τὰ μέλη τὰ ἐπὶ τῆς γῆς,

     Nekrōsate oun ta melē ta epi tēs gēs,

     Put to death, therefore, the earthly parts of you:

5b   πορνείαν, ἀκαθαρσίαν, πάθος, ἐπιθυμίαν κακήν,

     porneian, akatharsian, pathos, epithymian kakēn,

     καὶ τὴν πλεονεξίαν ἥτις ἐστὶν εἰδωλολατρία,

     kai tēn pleonexian hētis estin eidōlolatria,

     sexual immorality, impurity, lust, evil desires,
     and greed, which is idolatry.

6   δι’ ἃ ἔρχεται ἡ ὀργὴ τοῦ θεοῦ·

     di’ ha erchetai hē orgē tou theou;

     Because of these, the wrath of God is coming.

7a   ἐν οἷς καὶ ὑμεῖς περιεπατήσατέ ποτε

     en hois kai hymeis periepatēsate pote

     You also used to walk in these things,

7b   ὅτε ἐζῆτε ἐν τούτοις·

     hote ezēte en toutois;

     when you lived in them.

8a   νυνὶ δὲ ἀπόθεσθε καὶ ὑμεῖς τὰ πάντα,

     nyni de apothesthe kai hymeis ta panta,

     But now you also must throw off all these things,

8b   ὀργήν, θυμόν, κακίαν, βλασφημίαν,

     orgēn, thymon, kakian, blasphēmian,

     αἰσχρολογίαν ἐκ τοῦ στόματος ὑμῶν·

     aischrologian ek tou stomatos hymōn;

     anger, wrath, malice, slander,
     and obscene language from your mouth.

5a	**Νεκρώσατε οὖν τὰ μέλη τὰ ἐπὶ τῆς γῆς,**	
	Put to death, therefore, the earthly parts of you:	

Νεκρώσατε	(you all) put to death	AOR ACT IMPV	verb
νεκρόω	Ne·krō·sa·te	2ND PL	
οὖν	therefore	---	conj
οὖν	*oun*		
τὰ	the	ACC PL NEUT	article
ὁ	*ta*		
μέλη	parts	ACC PL NEUT	noun
μέλος	*me·lē*		
τὰ	the	ACC PL NEUT	article
ὁ	*ta*		
ἐπὶ	upon	---	prep
ἐπί	*e·pi*		
τῆς	the	GEN SG FEM	article
ὁ	*tēs*		
γῆς	earth	GEN SG FEM	noun
γῆ	*gēs*		

Νεκρώσατε ("put to death") is the first of three imperatives to come in 3:5–11. It looks back to both 3:1 and 2:20: because you have died with Christ, risen with Christ, and are with Christ in the heavenly realms, make your life reflect that reality. The things that once defined you when you were under the rule of earthly rulers in the kingdom of darkness should no longer exist.

5b	**πορνείαν, ἀκαθαρσίαν, πάθος, ἐπιθυμίαν κακήν,** **καὶ τὴν πλεονεξίαν ἥτις ἐστὶν εἰδωλολατρία,**	
	sexual immorality, impurity, lust, evil desires, and greed, which is idolatry.	

πορνείαν	sexual immorality	ACC SG FEM	noun
πορνεία	*por·nei·an*		
ἀκαθαρσίαν	impurity	ACC SG FEM	noun
ἀκαθαρσία	*a·ka·thar·si·an*		
πάθος	lust	ACC SG NEUT	noun
πάθος	*pa·thos*		
ἐπιθυμίαν	desire	ACC SG FEM	noun
ἐπιθυμία	*e·pi·thy·mi·an*		

κακήν κακός	evil *ka·kēn*	ACC SG FEM	adj
καὶ καί	and **kai**	---	conj
τὴν ὁ	the **tēn**	ACC SG FEM	article
πλεονεξίαν πλεονεξία	greed *ple·o·ne·**xi**·an*	ACC SG FEM	noun
ἥτις ὅστις	which **hē**·*tis*	NOM SG FEM	relative pron
ἐστὶν εἰμί	(it) is *e·**stin***	PRES ACT IND 3RD SG	verb
εἰδωλολατρία εἰδωλολατρία	idolatry *ei·dō·lo·la·**tri**·a*	NOM SG FEM	noun

---

6	δι' ἃ ἔρχεται ἡ ὀργὴ τοῦ θεοῦ·

Because of these, the wrath of God is coming.

δι' διά	because of *di'*	---	prep
ἃ ὅς	which (things) **ha**	ACC PL NEUT	relative pron
ἔρχεται ἔρχομαι	(it) comes *er·che·tai*	PRES MID IND 3RD SG	verb
ἡ ὁ	the *hē*	NOM SG FEM	article
ὀργὴ ὀργή	wrath *or·**gē***	NOM SG FEM	noun
τοῦ ὁ	of the **tou**	GEN SG MASC	article
θεοῦ θεός	(of) God *the·**ou***	GEN SG MASC	noun

7a	ἐν οἷς καὶ ὑμεῖς περιεπατήσατέ ποτε

You also used to walk in these things,

ἐν ἐν	in *en*	---	prep
οἷς ὅς	which (things) **hois**	DAT PL MASC	relative pron

καί καί	**and/also/even** *kai*	- - -	conj
ὑμεῖς σύ	**you (all)** *hy·meis*	2ND NOM PL	personal pron
περιεπατήσατέ περιπατέω	**(you all) walked** *pe·ri·e·pa·tē·sa·te*	AOR ACT IND 2ND PL	verb
ποτε ποτέ	**when/formerly** *po·te*	- - -	particle

This is the third time in this epistle that Paul uses the verb **περιπατέω** ("to walk") to describe the way in which the Colossians lived or should live (1:10; 2:6). They formerly "walked" in these vices (3:5, 8b) when they were enemies of God in their minds because of their evil behavior (1:21). At that time, they were under the rule of angelic powers and authorities in the kingdom of darkness, actively fighting against God (hence, "enemies" of God).

7b	**ὅτε ἐζῆτε ἐν τούτοις·**		
	when you lived in them.		
ὅτε ὅτε	**when** *ho·te*	- - -	adv
ἐζῆτε ζάω	**you (all) lived** *e·zē·te*	IMPF ACT IND 2ND PL	verb
ἐν ἐν	**in** *en*	- - -	prep
τούτοις οὗτος	**these (things)** *tou·tois*	DAT PL NEUT	demonst pron

Notice that Paul's language of participation works backwards as well as forwards. Now the believers live in Christ, in the kingdom of God; therefore, they must do the things that characterize participation in that realm. Formerly, however, they participated in the realm of the kingdom of darkness, and they participated *in the life of the things* that characterize that realm.

8a	**νυνὶ δὲ ἀπόθεσθε καὶ ὑμεῖς τὰ πάντα,**		
	But now you also must throw off all these things,		
νυνὶ νυνί	**now** *ny·ni*	- - -	adv

δὲ	but	---	conj
δέ	*de*		
ἀπόθεσθε	(you all) put away	AOR MID IMPV	verb
ἀποτίθημι	*a·po·the·sthe*	2ND PL	
καὶ	and/also	---	conj
καί	*kai*		
ὑμεῖς	you (all)	2ND NOM PL	personal
σύ	*hy·meis*		pron
τὰ	the	ACC PL NEUT	article
ὁ	*ta*		
πάντα	all (things)	ACC PL NEUT	adj
πᾶς	*pan·ta*		

Ἀπόθεσθε ("put away") is the second of three imperatives from 3:5–11. "Put away" or "rid yourself of" all these things, referring back to the vice list in 3:5 and anticipating the list that follows in 3:8b.

8b	**ὀργήν, θυμόν, κακίαν, βλασφημίαν, αἰσχρολογίαν ἐκ τοῦ στόματος ὑμῶν·**
	anger, wrath, malice, slander, and obscene language from your mouth.

ὀργήν	anger	ACC SG FEM	noun
ὀργή	*or·gēn*		
θυμόν	wrath	ACC SG MASC	noun
θυμός	*thy·mon*		
κακίαν	malice	ACC SG FEM	noun
κακία	*ka·ki·an*		
βλασφημίαν	slander	ACC SG FEM	noun
βλασφημία	*bla·sphē·mi·an*		
αἰσχρολογίαν	obscene language	ACC SG FEM	noun
αἰσχρολογία	*ai·schro·lo·gi·an*		
ἐκ	from	---	prep
ἐκ	*ek*		
τοῦ	the	GEN SG NEUT	article
ὁ	*tou*		
στόματος	mouth	GEN SG NEUT	noun
στόμα	*sto·ma·tos*		
ὑμῶν	of you (all)/your	2ND GEN PL	personal
σύ	*hy·mōn*		pron

9a

μὴ ψεύδεσθε εἰς ἀλλήλους·

mē pseudesthe eis allēlous;

Do not lie to one another;

9b

ἀπεκδυσάμενοι τὸν παλαιὸν ἄνθρωπον

apekdysamenoi ton palaion anthrōpon

you have stripped off the old self

9c

σὺν ταῖς πράξεσιν αὐτοῦ,

syn tais praxesin autou,

with its practices,

10a

καὶ ἐνδυσάμενοι τὸν νέον

kai endysamenoi ton neon

and have put on the new self,

10b

τὸν ἀνακαινούμενον εἰς ἐπίγνωσιν

ton anakainoumenon eis epignōsin

which is being renewed in knowledge

10c

κατ' εἰκόνα τοῦ κτίσαντος αὐτόν,

kat' eikona tou ktisantos auton,

according to the image of the one who created him,

11a

ὅπου οὐκ ἔνι Ἕλλην καὶ Ἰουδαῖος,

hopou ouk eni Hellēn kai Ioudaios,

where there is no Greek or Jew,

11b

περιτομὴ καὶ ἀκροβυστία,

peritomē kai akrobystia,

circumcision or uncircumcision,

11c	βάρβαρος, Σκύθης,
	barbaros, Skythēs,
	barbarian, Scythian,
11d	δοῦλος, ἐλεύθερος,
	doulos, eleutheros,
	slave or free,
11e	ἀλλὰ πάντα καὶ ἐν πᾶσιν Χριστός.
	alla panta kai en pasin Christos.
	but (the one who is) for all and in all is Christ.

9a	**μὴ ψεύδεσθε εἰς ἀλλήλους·**
	Do not lie to one another;

μὴ	not	---	particle
μή	*mē*		
ψεύδεσθε	(you all) lie	PRES MID IMPV	verb
ψεύδομαι	*pseu·de·sthe*	2ND PL	
εἰς	to	---	prep
εἰς	*eis*		
ἀλλήλους	one another	ACC PL MASC	reciprocal
ἀλλήλων	*al·lē·lous*		pron

The third imperative in 3:5–11 is **μή ψεύδεσθε** ("do not lie"). This phrase could be rendered "stop lying to one another," implying the present activity of lying, or "do not lie to one another," implying the possibility of lying, both in the present and future.

9b	**ἀπεκδυσάμενοι τὸν παλαιὸν ἄνθρωπον**
	you have stripped off the old self

ἀπεκδυσάμενοι	having discarded/disarmed	AOR MID PTCP	verb
ἀπεκδύομαι	*ap·ek·dy·sa·me·noi*	NOM PL MASC	

τὸν	the	ACC SG MASC	article
ὁ	*ton*		
παλαιὸν	old	ACC SG MASC	adj
παλαιός	*pa·lai·on*		
ἄνθρωπον	man/self	ACC SG MASC	noun
ἄνθρωπος	*an·thrō·pon*		

Most English translations translate the participle **ἀπεκδυσάμενοι** as "put off" (ESV, NKJV, RSV), "stripped off" (NRSV), or "taken off" (NIV). These are all appropriate, especially considering the use of **ἀποτίθημι** ("to take off" or "to do away with") in 3:8 and, more importantly, the coming parallel participle **ἐνδυσάμενοι** ("put on") in 3:10. Nonetheless, it is important to note that the word Paul uses here is the same word he uses in 2:15 to say that Christ "disarmed" the rulers and authorities on the cross. Also important is the fact that this word is only used in Col 2:15 and 3:9 in the entire New Testament and Septuagint (cf. the noun **ἀπεκδύσει** in 2:11). Within Paul's apocalyptic framework—particularly his understanding of salvation within that framework—it is likely that Paul is suggesting more than just a "stripping off" of the old self. That "old self was the enemy of God" (1:21). Paul's point here is that, when they were baptized into Christ, they died with Christ to their old nature, and were raised to new life in Christ with a new identity. In that process, they disarmed the power of the flesh, or the old self ruled by the flesh. They are now identified by Christ, the firstborn of the dead (1:18).

9c	**σὺν ταῖς πράξεσιν αὐτοῦ,**		
	with its practices,		
σὺν	with	---	prep
σύν	*syn*		
ταῖς	the (things)	DAT PL FEM	article
ὁ	*tais*		
πράξεσιν	deeds/practices	DAT PL FEM	noun
πρᾶξις	*pra·xe·sin*		
αὐτοῦ	of it	GEN SG MASC	personal
αὐτός	*au·tou*		pron

These are the same "practices" or "evil deeds" mentioned in 1:21.

	καὶ ἐνδυσάμενοι τὸν νέον		
	and have put on the new self		
καὶ	and	---	conj
καί	*kai*		
ἐνδυσάμενοι	having put on	AOR MID PTCP	verb
ἐνδύω	*en·dy·sa·me·noi*	NOM PL MASC	
τὸν	the	ACC SG MASC	article
ὁ	*ton*		
νέον	new (one)	ACC SG MASC	adj
νέος	*ne·on*		

Though Paul does not elaborate here on his Adam-Christ typology, the attentive reader can certainly make connections to what he writes in Rom 5:12–21; 8:29; and 1 Cor 15:20–28. To "put on the new self" is to put on the new Adam, the firstborn from the dead (1:18), who is also the image of the invisible God, the firstborn over all creation (1:15).

	τὸν ἀνακαινούμενον εἰς ἐπίγνωσιν		
	which is being renewed in knowledge		
τὸν	the	ACC SG MASC	article
ὁ	*ton*		
ἀνακαινούμενον	(one) being made new	PRES PASS PTCP	verb
ἀνακαινόω	*a·na·kai·nou·me·non*	ACC SG MASC	
εἰς	into	---	prep
εἰς	*eis*		
ἐπίγνωσιν	knowledge	ACC SG FEM	noun
ἐπίγνωσις	*e·pi·gnō·sin*		

	κατ' εἰκόνα τοῦ κτίσαντος αὐτόν,		
	according to the image of the one who created him,		
κατ'	according to	---	prep
κατά	*kat'*		
εἰκόνα	image	ACC SG FEM	noun
εἰκών	*ei·ko·na*		
τοῦ	of the	GEN SG MASC	article
ὁ	*tou*		
κτίσαντος	of (one) having created	AOR ACT PTCP	verb
κτίζω	*kti·san·tos*	GEN SG MASC	

αὐτόν	him	ACC SG MASC	personal
αὐτός	*au·ton*		pron

The emphasis on the contrast between the first Adam and the new Adam becomes evident in the image language used here. The first human, made in the image of God in Gen 1:26–28, capitulated to evil powers and became corrupt. That corrupt human self is now "stripped off" and disarmed; more importantly, the new self is being renewed in the image of Christ, who is the image of the invisible God himself (Col 1:15).

11a	ὅπου οὐκ ἔνι Ἕλλην καὶ Ἰουδαῖος,
	where there is no Greek or Jew,

ὅπου	where	---	adv
ὅπου	*ho·pou*		
οὐκ	no	---	particle
οὐ	*ouk*		
ἔνι	(it) exists	PRES ACT IND 3RD SG	verb
ἔνειμι	*e·ni*		
Ἕλλην	Greek	NOM SG MASC	noun
Ἕλλην	*Hel·lēn*		
καὶ	and	---	conj
καί	*kai*		
Ἰουδαῖος	Jewish (one)	NOM SG MASC	adj
Ἰουδαῖος	*I·ou·dai·os*		

11b	περιτομὴ καὶ ἀκροβυστία,
	circumcision or uncircumcision,

περιτομὴ	circumcision	NOM SG FEM	noun
περιτομή	*pe·ri·to·mē*		
καὶ	and	---	conj
καί	*kai*		
ἀκροβυστία	uncircumcision	NOM SG FEM	noun
ἀκροβυστία	*a·kro·by·sti·a*		

11c	βάρβαρος, Σκύθης,		
	barbarian, Scythian,		
βάρβαρος βάρβαρος	barbarous (one) *bar·bar·os*	NOM SG MASC	adj
Σκύθης Σκύθης	Scythian *Sky·thēs*	NOM SG MASC	noun

11d	δοῦλος, ἐλεύθερος,		
	slave or free,		
δοῦλος δοῦλος	slave *dou·los*	NOM SG MASC	noun
ἐλεύθερος ἐλεύθερος	free (one) *e·leu·the·ros*	NOM SG MASC	adj

11e	ἀλλὰ πάντα καὶ ἐν πᾶσιν Χριστός.		
	but the one who is for all and in all is Christ.		
ἀλλὰ ἀλλά	but *al·la*	---	conj
πάντα πᾶς	all (things) *pan·ta*	NOM PL NEUT	adj
καὶ καί	and *kai*	---	conj
ἐν ἐν	in *en*	---	prep
πᾶσιν πᾶς	all (things) *pa·sin*	DAT PL NEUT	adj
Χριστός Χριστός	Christ *Chri·stos*	NOM SG MASC	noun

The **πάντα** here is a predicate nominative, and as such it completes the clause: Christ is everything. The beauty of this verse, in addition to its high Christology, is that **Χριστός** ("Christ") comes at the very end, both of this verse and also of this long section of focusing on the believers' new life in Christ that began in 2:1. The focus from start to finish is on the resurrection life *in Christ*, the very Christ who reconciled believers from all backgrounds to be identified first and foremost in him, the new human and the image of the invisible God.

12a
Ἐνδύσασθε οὖν ὡς ἐκλεκτοὶ τοῦ θεοῦ,

Endysasthe oun hōs eklektoi tou theou,

Put on, therefore, as chosen ones of God,

12b
ἅγιοι καὶ ἠγαπημένοι,

hagioi kai ēgapēmenoi,

holy and beloved,

12c
σπλάγχνα οἰκτιρμοῦ,

splanchna oiktirmou,

hearts of compassion,

12d
χρηστότητα, ταπεινοφροσύνην, πραΰτητα, μακροθυμίαν,

chrēstotēta, tapeinophrosynēn, praytēta, makrothymian,

kindness, humility, gentleness, and patience.

13a
ἀνεχόμενοι ἀλλήλων

anechomenoi allēlōn

Bear with each other,

13b
καὶ χαριζόμενοι ἑαυτοῖς

kai charizomenoi heautois

and forgive one another

13c
ἐάν τις πρός τινα ἔχῃ μομφήν·

ean tis pros tina echē momphēn;

when you have a complaint against another;

13d
καθὼς καὶ ὁ κύριος ἐχαρίσατο ὑμῖν

kathōs kai ho kyrios echarisato hymin

just as the Lord forgave you,

13e

οὕτως καὶ ὑμεῖς·

houtōs kai hymeis;

you also should forgive one another.

14a

ἐπὶ πᾶσι δὲ τούτοις τὴν ἀγάπην,

epi pasi de toutois tēn agapēn,

And over all these things put on love,

14b

ὅ ἐστιν σύνδεσμος τῆς τελειότητος.

ho estin syndesmos tēs teleiotētos.

which is the bond of perfect unity.

12a	Ἐνδύσασθε οὖν ὡς ἐκλεκτοὶ τοῦ θεοῦ,		
	Put on, therefore, as chosen ones of God,		
Ἐνδύσασθε ἐνδύω	(you all) put on *En · dy · sa · sthe*	AOR MID IMPV 2ND PL	verb
οὖν οὖν	therefore *oun*	---	conj
ὡς ὡς	as *hōs*	---	adv
ἐκλεκτοὶ ἐκλεκτός	chosen (ones) *ek · le · ktoi*	NOM PL MASC	adj
τοῦ ὁ	of the *tou*	GEN SG MASC	article
θεοῦ θεός	(of) God *the · ou*	GEN SG MASC	noun

Ἐνδύσασθε ("put on") is the same word we saw in 3:10, where the focus was on the renewal of our selves in the image of Christ. Here Paul gives the specific virtues that must come with such renewal in Christ. Whereas in 3:5–11 the focus was on the vices to be eradicated, in 3:12–17 the focus is on the virtues that ought to replace them.

12b — ἅγιοι καὶ ἠγαπημένοι,

holy and beloved,

ἅγιοι ἅγιος	holy (ones) *ha·gi·oi*	NOM PL MASC	adj
καὶ καί	and *kai*	---	conj
ἠγαπημένοι ἀγαπάω	(ones) having been loved *ē·ga·pē·me·noi*	PERF PASS PTCP NOM PL MASC	verb

12c — σπλάγχνα οἰκτιρμοῦ,

hearts of compassion,

σπλάγχνα σπλάγχνον	bowels/hearts *splan·chna*	ACC PL NEUT	noun
οἰκτιρμοῦ οἰκτιρμός	of compassion *oi·ktir·mou*	GEN SG MASC	noun

12d — χρηστότητα, ταπεινοφροσύνην, πραΰτητα, μακροθυμίαν,

kindness, humility, gentleness, and patience.

χρηστότητα χρηστότης	kindness *chrē·sto·tē·ta*	ACC SG FEM	noun
ταπεινοφροσύνην ταπεινοφροσύνη	humility *ta·pei·no·phro·sy·nēn*	ACC SG FEM	noun
πραΰτητα πραΰτης	gentleness *pra·y·tē·ta*	ACC SG FEM	noun
μακροθυμίαν μακροθυμία	patience *ma·kro·thy·mi·an*	ACC SG FEM	noun

13a — ἀνεχόμενοι ἀλλήλων

Bear with each other

ἀνεχόμενοι ἀνέχομαι	bearing *an·e·cho·me·noi*	PRES MID PTCP NOM PL MASC	verb
ἀλλήλων ἀλλήλων	of one another *al·lē·lōn*	GEN PL MASC	reciprocal pron

13b

καὶ χαριζόμενοι ἑαυτοῖς

and forgive one another

καὶ καί	and *kai*	---	conj
χαριζόμενοι χαρίζομαι	forgiving *cha·ri·zo·me·noi*	PRES MID PTCP NOM PL MASC	verb
ἑαυτοῖς ἑαυτοῦ	themselves *he·au·tois*	2ND DAT PL MASC	reflexive pron

13c

ἐάν τις πρός τινα ἔχῃ μομφήν·

when you have a complaint against another;

ἐάν ἐάν	if *e·an*	---	cond
τις τίς	anyone *tis*	NOM SG MASC	indef pron
πρός πρός	toward *pros*	---	prep
τινα τίς	anyone *ti·na*	ACC SG MASC	indef pron
ἔχῃ ἔχω	(he/she) should have *e·chē*	PRES ACT SUBJ 3RD SG	verb
μομφήν μομφή	complaint *mom·phēn*	ACC SG FEM	noun

13d

καθὼς καὶ ὁ κύριος ἐχαρίσατο ὑμῖν

just as the Lord forgave you,

καθὼς καθώς	just as *ka·thōs*	---	adv
καὶ καί	also/even *kai*	---	conj
ὁ ὁ	the *ho*	NOM SG MASC	article
κύριος κύριος	Lord *ky·ri·os*	NOM SG MASC	noun
ἐχαρίσατο χαρίζομαι	(he) forgave *e·cha·ri·sa·to*	AOR MID IND 3RD SG	verb
ὑμῖν σύ	you (all) *hy·min*	2ND DAT PL	personal pron

13e — οὕτως καὶ ὑμεῖς·

you also should forgive one another.

Greek	Gloss	Parsing	Type
οὕτως οὕτως	thus *hou·tōs*	---	adv
καὶ καί	also *kai*	---	conj
ὑμεῖς σύ	you (all) *hy·meis*	2ND NOM PL	personal pron

Though this final "should forgive one another" is not explicit in the Greek, it is clearly implied.

14a — ἐπὶ πᾶσι δὲ τούτοις τὴν ἀγάπην,

And over all these things put on love,

Greek	Gloss	Parsing	Type
ἐπὶ ἐπί	upon *e·pi*	---	prep
πᾶσι πᾶς	all (things) *pa·si*	DAT PL NEUT	adj
δὲ δέ	and *de*	---	conj
τούτοις οὗτος	these *tou·tois*	DAT PL NEUT	demonstr pron
τὴν ὁ	the *tēn*	ACC SG FEM	article
ἀγάπην ἀγάπη	love *a·ga·pēn*	ACC SG FEM	noun

Ἐνδύσασθε ("put on") is carried forward from 3:12 to here.

14b — ὅ ἐστιν σύνδεσμος τῆς τελειότητος.

which is the bond of perfect unity.

Greek	Gloss	Parsing	Type
ὅ ὅς	which *ho*	NOM SG NEUT	relative pron
ἐστιν εἰμί	(it) is *e·stin*	PRES ACT IND 3RD SG	verb
σύνδεσμος σύνδεσμος	bond *syn·de·smos*	NOM SG MASC	noun

τῆς	of the	GEN SG FEM	article
ὁ	*tēs*		
τελειότητος	(of) completeness	GEN SG FEM	noun
τελειότης	*te·lei·o·tē·tos*		

While **τελειότης** denotes "completeness" or "perfection," Paul's focus here is on corporate harmony and unity as the body of Christ. Love for one another is the glue that bonds believers together.

15a
καὶ ἡ εἰρήνη τοῦ χριστοῦ βραβευέτω

kai hē eirēnē tou christou brabeuetō

And let the peace of Christ rule

15b
ἐν ταῖς καρδίαις ὑμῶν,

en tais kardiais hymōn,

in your hearts,

15c
εἰς ἣν καὶ ἐκλήθητε ἐν ἑνὶ σώματι·

eis hēn kai eklēthēte en heni sōmati;

to which indeed you were called in one body;

15d
καὶ εὐχάριστοι γίνεσθε.

kai eucharistoi ginesthe.

and be thankful.

16a
ὁ λόγος τοῦ χριστοῦ ἐνοικείτω ἐν ὑμῖν πλουσίως,

ho logos tou christou enoikeitō en hymin plousiōs,

Let the word of Christ dwell in you richly,

16b
ἐν πάσῃ σοφίᾳ διδάσκοντες καὶ νουθετοῦντες ἑαυτούς,

en pasē sophia didaskontes kai nouthetountes heautous,

teaching and admonishing one another in all wisdom,

16c
ψαλμοῖς, ὕμνοις, ᾠδαῖς πνευματικαῖς

psalmois, hymnois, ōdais pneumatikais

in psalms, hymns, and spiritual songs,

16d
ἐν χάριτι, ᾄδοντες ἐν ταῖς καρδίαις ὑμῶν τῷ θεῷ·

en chariti, adontes en tais kardiais hymōn tō theō;

singing with thankfulness in your hearts to God.

17a

καὶ πᾶν ὅ τι ἐὰν ποιῆτε ἐν λόγῳ ἢ ἐν ἔργῳ,

kai pan ho ti ean poiēte en logō ē en ergō,

And whatever you do, whether in word or deed,

17b

πάντα ἐν ὀνόματι κυρίου Ἰησοῦ,

panta en onomati kyriou Iēsou,

do everything in the name of the Lord Jesus,

17c

εὐχαριστοῦντες τῷ θεῷ πατρὶ δι᾽ αὐτοῦ.

eucharistountes tō theō patri di᾽ autou.

giving thanks to God the Father through him.

15a	**καὶ ἡ εἰρήνη τοῦ χριστοῦ βραβευέτω**		
	And let the peace of Christ rule		
καὶ καί	and *kai*	---	conj
ἡ ὁ	the *hē*	NOM SG FEM	article
εἰρήνη εἰρήνη	peace *ei·rē·nē*	NOM SG FEM	noun
τοῦ ὁ	of the *tou*	GEN SG MASC	article
χριστοῦ Χριστός	(of) Christ *chri·stou*	GEN SG MASC	noun
βραβευέτω βραβεύω	let (it) rule *bra·beu·e·tō*	PRES ACT IMPV 3RD SG	verb

As was mentioned at 1:2, this "peace" of Christ is not inner tranquility but rather a sense of justness and rightness. In contrast to the evil that once *ruled* their hearts within the kingdom of darkness, now peace *rules* their hearts as those whose identity is in the kingdom of the Son. The use of βραβεύω ("to rule"), which is found only here in the New Testament, implies an element of "judging" or "presiding."

15b	ἐν ταῖς καρδίαις ὑμῶν,		
	in your hearts,		
ἐν	in	---	prep
ἐν	*en*		
ταῖς	the	DAT PL FEM	article
ὁ	*tais*		
καρδίαις	hearts	DAT PL FEM	noun
καρδία	*kar·di·ais*		
ὑμῶν	of you (all)/your	2ND GEN PL	personal
σύ	*hy·mōn*		pron

15c	εἰς ἣν καὶ ἐκλήθητε ἐν ἑνὶ σώματι·		
	to which indeed you were called in one body;		
εἰς	for	---	prep
εἰς	*eis*		
ἣν	which	ACC SG FEM	relative
ὅς	*hēn*		pron
καὶ	also/even	---	conj
καί	*kai*		
ἐκλήθητε	you (all) were called	AOR PASS IND	verb
καλέω	*ek·lē·thē·te*	2ND PL	
ἐν	in	---	prep
ἐν	*en*		
ἑνὶ	one	DAT SG NEUT	adj
εἷς	*he·ni*		
σώματι	body	DAT SG NEUT	noun
σῶμα	*sō·ma·ti*		

15d	καὶ εὐχάριστοι γίνεσθε.		
	and be thankful.		
καὶ	and	---	conj
καί	*kai*		
εὐχάριστοι	thankful (ones)	NOM PL MASC	adj
εὐχάριστος	*eu·cha·ri·stoi*		
γίνεσθε	(you all) be	PRES MID IMPV	verb
γίνομαι	*gi·ne·sthe*	2ND PL	

ὁ λόγος τοῦ χριστοῦ ἐνοικείτω ἐν ὑμῖν πλουσίως,

Let the word of Christ dwell in you richly,

ὁ ὁ	the *ho*	NOM SG MASC	article
λόγος λόγος	word *lo·gos*	NOM SG MASC	noun
τοῦ ὁ	of the *tou*	GEN SG MASC	article
χριστοῦ Χριστός	(of) Christ *chri·stou*	GEN SG MASC	noun
ἐνοικείτω ἐνοικέω	let (it) dwell *en·oi·kei·tō*	PRES ACT IMPV 3RD SG	verb
ἐν ἐν	in *en*	---	prep
ὑμῖν σύ	you (all) *hy·min*	2ND DAT PL	personal pron
πλουσίως πλουσίως	richly *plou·si·ōs*	---	adv

ἐν πάσῃ σοφίᾳ διδάσκοντες καὶ νουθετοῦντες ἑαυτούς,

teaching and admonishing one another in all wisdom,

ἐν ἐν	in *en*	---	prep
πάσῃ πᾶς	all *pa·sē*	DAT SG FEM	adj
σοφίᾳ σοφία	wisdom *so·phi·a*	DAT SG FEM	noun
διδάσκοντες διδάσκω	teaching *di·da·skon·tes*	PRES ACT PTCP NOM PL MASC	verb
καὶ καί	and *kai*	---	conj
νουθετοῦντες νουθετέω	admonishing *nou·the·toun·tes*	PRES ACT PTCP NOM PL MASC	verb
ἑαυτούς ἑαυτοῦ	themselves *he·au·tous*	2ND ACC PL MASC	reflexive pron

in psalms, hymns, and spiritual songs,

ψαλμοῖς ψαλμός	(in/with/by) psalms psal·**mois**	DAT PL MASC	noun
ὕμνοις ὕμνος	(in/with/by) hymns hy·mnois	DAT PL MASC	noun
ᾠδαῖς ᾠδή	(in/with/by) songs ō·**dais**	DAT PL FEM	noun
πνευματικαῖς πνευματικός	spiritual pneu·ma·ti·**kais**	DAT PL FEM	adj

Due to the format of the Greek at this point, the most natural translation would be to keep **ᾄδοντες** ("singing") with 16c, so that the longer clause reads "singing psalms, hymns, and spiritual songs, with thankfulness in your hearts to God." In this case, because in this volume we are showing the text according to its sub-clauses, it works well enough to include "in" at the start of the clause in 16c, which renders it only slightly less smooth.

singing with thankfulness in your hearts to God.

ἐν ἐν	with en	---	prep
χάριτι χάρις	grace cha·ri·ti	DAT SG FEM	noun
ᾄδοντες ᾄδω	singing a·don·tes	PRES ACT PTCP NOM PL MASC	verb
ἐν ἐν	in en	---	prep
ταῖς ὁ	the tais	DAT PL FEM	article
καρδίαις καρδία	hearts kar·di·ais	DAT PL FEM	noun
ὑμῶν σύ	of you (all)/your hy·**mōn**	2ND GEN PL	personal pron
τῷ ὁ	to the tō	DAT SG MASC	article
θεῷ θεός	God the·ō	DAT SG MASC	noun

καὶ πᾶν ὅ τι ἐὰν ποιῆτε ἐν λόγῳ ἢ ἐν ἔργῳ,

And whatever you do, whether in word or deed,

Greek	Gloss	Parsing	POS
καὶ καί	and *kai*	---	conj
πᾶν πᾶς	all *pan*	ACC SG NEUT	adj
ὅ ὁ	that/which *ho*	NOM SG MASC	rel pron
τι τίς	anyone *ti*	ACC SG NEUT	indef pron
ἐὰν ἐάν	if *e·an*	---	cond
ποιῆτε ποιέω	(you all) might do *poi·ē·te*	PRES ACT SUBJ 2ND PL	verb
ἐν ἐν	in *en*	---	prep
λόγῳ λόγος	word *lo·gō*	DAT SG MASC	noun
ἤ ἤ	or *ē*	---	particle
ἐν ἐν	in *en*	---	prep
ἔργῳ ἔργον	deed *er·gō*	DAT SG NEUT	noun

πάντα ἐν ὀνόματι κυρίου Ἰησοῦ,

do everything in the name of the Lord Jesus,

Greek	Gloss	Parsing	POS
πάντα πᾶς	all (things) *pan·ta*	ACC PL NEUT	adj
ἐν ἐν	in *en*	---	prep
ὀνόματι ὄνομα	name *o·no·ma·ti*	DAT SG NEUT	noun
κυρίου κύριος	of Lord *ky·ri·ou*	GEN SG MASC	noun
Ἰησοῦ Ἰησοῦς	(of) Jesus *I·ē·sou*	GEN SG MASC	noun

εὐχαριστοῦντες τῷ θεῷ πατρὶ δι᾽ αὐτοῦ.

giving thanks to God the Father through him.

εὐχαριστοῦντες εὐχαριστέω	giving thanks *eu·cha·ri·stoun·tes*	PRES ACT PTCP NOM PL MASC	verb
τῷ ὁ	to the *tō*	DAT SG MASC	article
θεῷ θεός	God *the·ō*	DAT SG MASC	noun
πατρὶ πατήρ	father *pa·tri*	DAT SG MASC	noun
δι᾽ διά	through/because of *di᾽*	---	prep
αὐτοῦ αὐτός	him *au·tou*	GEN SG MASC	personal pron

Big Idea. Your new identity is in Christ, so let your life make that obvious in your relationships with everyone.

 Bridge to Theology. For Paul, this transfer from the kingdom of darkness to the kingdom of the Son marks a shift in our very being, our truest identity. Who we are in that fundamental identity is demonstrated by how we live, both as individuals and in relationship with others. We formerly were participants in the kingdom of darkness, which was evidenced by the vices that we exhibited. But now we are *in Christ* in the heavenly realms within the kingdom of God. Therefore, our actions, attitudes, perspectives, and relationships ought to reflect that new and true identity. We ought to live with one another in unity, having relationships characterized by peace, kindness, patience, forgiveness, and love. Why? Because we are *in Christ* and in him there is no evil or darkness. What is true of him is true of us, so we ought to live out that reality.

 Illustrations/Applications. Whereas in the previous passage the emphasis was on the way in which the church was being shaped through external factors, such as human-made religious regulations, now the emphasis is on how the church is shaped from within, through the actions and relationships among its members. One obvious option for helping your congregants think through this passage is to have them think about the ways in which they have allowed their own vices of the past, the things that characterize a non-Christian life, to have a role in who they are today. What has carried over? What vice has been difficult to "put to death?" Why? What is feeding that vice? What forms of accountability have they established? These might be some questions to ask.

Another question might be, "What Christ-like characteristics has God shaped in you?" Are you practicing humility? Compassion? Patience? And how are these demonstrated in your relationships? What about within your home—are you demonstrating patience with your children, or humility with your spouse, or kindness toward your roommate? What about in your work environment—are you demonstrating gentleness with coworkers? What about in the ways you have been called to lead—are you doing so with gentleness and kindness? And what about within the congregation—what does the unity of your church look like? Are there grievances among the members of the church? Perhaps there is a particular relationship that needs some additional assistance in order to bring about reconciliation. (I remember being at a seminar once where an attendee asked Tom Wright what one critique he thinks Paul would give the church today. Tom's answer was that Paul would say the church has failed in its number one objective: to be united as the body of Christ.) Church unity is something Paul cared about deeply. Perhaps your church, as well as most others, could use a bit of a refresher on its importance.

HOUSEHOLD RELATIONSHIPS

Life in the kingdom of the Son is about unity within the church, but it is also about right relationships within the household. How a husband, for example, treats his wife or his children will ultimately bear witness to the lordship of Christ and the transforming power of the gospel in the world around him. This, in part, is how the gospel will continue to bear fruit in the world (1:6) and how the Colossian Christians may "live in a manner worthy of the Lord, pleasing him in every way" (1:10).

18a   Αἱ γυναῖκες, ὑποτάσσεσθε τοῖς ἀνδράσιν,

Hai gynaikes, hypotassesthe tois andrasin,

Wives, submit to your husbands

18b   ὡς ἀνῆκεν ἐν κυρίῳ.

hōs anēken en kyriō.

as is befitting in the Lord.

19a   Οἱ ἄνδρες, ἀγαπᾶτε τὰς γυναῖκας

Hoi andres, agapate tas gynaikas

Husbands, love your wives,

19b   καὶ μὴ πικραίνεσθε πρὸς αὐτάς.

kai mē pikrainesthe pros autas.

and do not be harsh toward them.

20a   Τὰ τέκνα, ὑπακούετε τοῖς γονεῦσιν κατὰ πάντα,

Ta tekna, hypakouete tois goneusin kata panta,

Children, obey your parents in all things,

20b   τοῦτο γὰρ εὐάρεστόν ἐστιν ἐν κυρίῳ.

touto gar euareston estin en kyriō.

for this pleases the Lord.

21a   Οἱ πατέρες, μὴ ἐρεθίζετε τὰ τέκνα ὑμῶν,

Hoi pateres, mē erethizete ta tekna hymōn,

Fathers, do not embitter your children,

21b   ἵνα μὴ ἀθυμῶσιν.

hina mē athymōsin.

lest they become discouraged.

Αἱ γυναῖκες, ὑποτάσσεσθε τοῖς ἀνδράσιν,

Wives, submit to your husbands

Greek	English	Parsing	Type
Αἱ ὁ	the *Hai*	NOM PL FEM	article
γυναῖκες γυνή	wives *gy·**nai**·kes*	NOM PL FEM	noun
ὑποτάσσεσθε ὑποτάσσω	(you all) submit yourselves *hy·po·**tas**·se·sthe*	PRES MID IMPV 2ND PL	verb
τοῖς ὁ	to the *tois*	DAT PL MASC	article
ἀνδράσιν ἀνήρ	husbands *an·**dra**·sin*	DAT PL MASC	noun

This passage from 3:18 to 4:1 is notoriously difficult to translate, interpret, and to know how to apply to Christian life in the twenty-first century. As many are aware, Paul's words have been misused and abused in a multitude of ways, from misogyny, to various forms of spousal and child abuse, to condoning slavery, and to any number of forms of oppression against marginalized groups. While there is limited space in this volume to do a deep dive of any of these verses, what can be said definitively is that Paul never endorsed any form of injustice or oppression against women, children, or those in otherwise vulnerable positions. For Paul, as seen already in Colossians, the Christian life is a cruciform life—a life lived in support of, in solidarity with, and in service to the suffering, the marginalized, and the oppressed. To live in the kingdom of God, to be alive in Christ, is to live a life of love. This cruciform life also leads one to lament. One way to show solidarity with the suffering of the vulnerable is to lament that suffering happens at all in God's good creation, and especially to lament the fact that texts such as this one have been used to create and promote such suffering. Therefore, in comments on this section, I will dedicate space to highlight the key lexical and semantic issues at play, and when appropriate, direct the reader to other helpful secondary sources.

The second word, **γυναῖκες**, can mean either "women" or "wives." Similarly, the final word, **ἀνδράσιν**, can mean either "men" or "husbands." A substantial difference is immediately apparent if the words "women" and "men" are chosen. Does Paul really mean to say that *all women* are to be subject to *all men*? Given that the larger context of this passage focuses on relationships within a first-century household, the more likely translation includes "wives" and "husbands."

The critical word in this clause is **ὑποτάσσεσθε**, a word used only here in Colossians but fairly frequently throughout the rest of Paul's letters. It can mean "bring into compliance" or "subject" or "submit," depending on the context. Several important points can be made about Paul's use of this term here. The first is that it is in the middle "voice," which means that it is an action carried out by the wife herself—she decides to be submissive; she is not obligated to do so. The second thing to note is that the word means "submission," generally speaking, and not "obedience" (ὑπακούω, which he uses in 3:20) or "subservience." The third thing to note is that it is the same word Paul uses in Eph 5:21, where he tells both the wife and the husband to *submit to one another* (a phrase that ought to be connected to 5:22ff. rather than 5:20 and previous). Fourth, we must keep everything in mind that Paul has said in Colossians up to this point, namely that all believers are in Christ, have had their entire existence transformed by their baptismal transformation into Christ, and this new reality (see esp. Col 3:11) is what shapes every element of their lives, especially their relationships with one another, including those within the household.

For a detailed analysis of the complexities associated with 3:18–19, I recommend Scot McKnight's *The Letter to the Colossians* (2018), and for a broader understanding of the larger themes of gender in Paul's letters, see Cynthia Long Westfall's *Paul and Gender: Reclaiming the Apostle's Vision for Men and Women in Christ* (2016).

18b	ὡς ἀνῆκεν ἐν κυρίῳ.		
	as is fitting in the Lord.		
ὡς ὡς	as hōs	---	adv
ἀνῆκεν ἀνήκω	(it) is fitting a·nē·ken	IMPF ACT IND 3RD SG	verb
ἐν ἐν	in en	---	prep
κυρίῳ κύριος	Lord ky·ri·ō	DAT SG MASC	noun

The use of ἀνῆκεν ("fitting" or "proper") here is one of three appearances in Paul's letters (see also Eph 5:4 and Phlm 8). The word is used in contexts where the emphasis is on the life of the believer in the name of the Lord Jesus (Col 3:17) or in the kingdom of God (Eph 5:5) or in partnership in the gospel (Phlm 6). This whole section of 3:18—4:1 is Paul's commentary on what household relationships ought to look like if one truly lives their lives "in the name of the Lord Jesus" (3:17). Here he simply restates "in the name of the Lord Jesus" with "in the Lord." The truly transformed life ought to be evident in one's relationships, especially those within the household.

19a	**Οἱ ἄνδρες, ἀγαπᾶτε τὰς γυναῖκας**		
	Husbands, love your wives,		
Οἱ ὁ	the *Hoi*	NOM PL MASC	article
ἄνδρες ἀνήρ	husbands *an·dres*	NOM PL MASC	noun
ἀγαπᾶτε ἀγαπάω	(you all) love *a·ga·**pa**·te*	PRES ACT IMPV 2ND PL	verb
τὰς ὁ	the *tas*	ACC PL FEM	article
γυναῖκας γυνή	wives *gy·**nai**·kas*	ACC PL FEM	noun

This command to husbands to love their wives is countercultural within the Roman empire. Paul is not telling the Colossians to live according to the cultural norms of marital hierarchies; on the contrary, he challenges those hierarchies in light of the rule of Christ. Moreover, he has just said in Col 3:14 that it is love that is the greatest of the virtues. How can one know if a person is dead to sin and alive to God in Christ? They demonstrate the love of Christ in their relationships.

19b	**καὶ μὴ πικραίνεσθε πρὸς αὐτάς.**		
	and do not be harsh toward them.		
καὶ καί	and *kai*	---	conj
μὴ μή	not *mē*	---	particle
πικραίνεσθε πικραίνω	(you all) be embittered *pi·**krai**·ne·sthe*	PRES PASS IMPV 2ND PL	verb
πρὸς πρός	toward *pros*	---	prep
αὐτάς αὐτός	them *au·**tas***	ACC PL FEM	personal pron

Most modern translations use either "harsh" or "embittered" to render **πικραίνεσθε**. The word is found only here and three times in Revelation

(8:11; 10:9, 10), where it is clearly indicates a "bitter" taste. It might be that Paul is telling the Colossian husbands not to be bitter toward their wives, or it can be a figurative use of the word, indicating something more like "harsh treatment." This feels only slightly more likely, given that it is in contrast to the "love" they ought to show from the previous clause.

20a	Τὰ τέκνα, ὑπακούετε τοῖς γονεῦσιν κατὰ πάντα,		
	Children, obey your parents in all things,		
Τὰ ὁ	the *Ta*	NOM PL NEUT	article
τέκνα τέκνον	children *te·kna*	NOM PL NEUT	noun
ὑπακούετε ὑπακούω	(you all) obey *hyp·a·kou·e·te*	PRES ACT IMPV 2ND PL	verb
τοῖς ὁ	(to) the *tois*	DAT PL MASC	article
γονεῦσιν γονεύς	parents *go·neu·sin*	DAT PL MASC	noun
κατὰ κατά	according to *ka·ta*	---	prep
πάντα πᾶς	all (things) *pan·ta*	ACC PL NEUT	adj

Children were generally expected to obey their parents in the first-century Roman world, whether they were of a Jewish or Hellenistic background. In his use of **κατὰ πάντα** ("all things"), Paul does not suggest that the child is expected to obey a parent even when the expectations are unreasonable or unjust (i.e., at all times). The idea is rather that, as those who are in Christ, their general disposition will be one of humility, service, love, and obedience.

20b	τοῦτο γὰρ εὐάρεστόν ἐστιν ἐν κυρίῳ.		
	for this pleases the Lord.		
τοῦτο οὗτος	this *tou·to*	NOM SG NEUT	demonstr pron
γὰρ γάρ	for *gar*	---	conj
εὐάρεστόν εὐάρεστος	pleasing *eu·a·re·ston*	NOM SG NEUT	adj

ἐστιν	(it) is	PRES ACT IND	verb
εἰμί	*e·stin*	3RD SG	
ἐν	in	---	prep
ἐν	*en*		
κυρίῳ	Lord	DAT SG MASC	noun
κύριος	*ky·ri·ō*		

Note that the literal translation here would be "for this is pleasing *in the Lord*," again emphasizing the new life of love is a result of a transformed life in Christ. This transformation is equally as real for a child in Christ as it is for an adult in Christ.

21a	**Οἱ πατέρες, μὴ ἐρεθίζετε τὰ τέκνα ὑμῶν,**		
	Fathers, do not embitter your children,		
Οἱ	the	NOM PL MASC	article
ὁ	*Hoi*		
πατέρες	fathers	NOM PL MASC	noun
πατήρ	*pa·te·res*		
μὴ	not	---	particle
μή	*mē*		
ἐρεθίζετε	(you all) embitter	PRES ACT IMPV	verb
ἐρεθίζω	*e·re·thi·ze·te*	2ND PL	
τὰ	the	ACC PL NEUT	article
ὁ	*ta*		
τέκνα	children	ACC PL NEUT	noun
τέκνον	*te·kna*		
ὑμῶν	of you (all)/your	2ND GEN PL	personal
σύ	*hy·mōn*		pron

Note that Paul's word for "embitter" here is different from what he used in 3:19 to refer to a husband's treatment of his wife. The word here, **ἐρεθίζετε**, can have a number of meanings, including "embitter," "vex," "challenge," and "incite." It is found only here and in 2 Cor 9:2, where it is used in a similar way.

21b	**ἵνα μὴ ἀθυμῶσιν.**		
	lest they become discouraged.		
ἵνα	in order that	---	conj
ἵνα	*hi·na*		

μὴ	not	---	particle
μή	*mē*		
ἀθυμῶσιν	(they) might be discouraged	PRES ACT SUBJ 3RD PL	verb
ἀθυμέω	*a·thy·mō·sin*		

3:22a

Οἱ δοῦλοι, ὑπακούετε κατὰ πάντα

*Hoi **douloi**, hypa**kouete ka**ta **panta***

τοῖς κατὰ σάρκα κυρίοις,

***tois ka**ta **sarka** kyriois,*

Slaves, obey your earthly masters in everything,

3:22b

μὴ ἐν ὀφθαλμοδουλίαις,

mē en ophthalmodouliais,

not only when they are watching,

3:22c

ὡς ἀνθρωπάρεσκοι,

*hōs anthrō**pareskoi**,*

as people pleasers,

3:22d

ἀλλ' ἐν ἁπλότητι καρδίας,

*all' en ha**plo**tēti kar**di**as,*

but with sincerity of heart,

22e

φοβούμενοι τὸν κύριον.

*pho**bou**menoi **ton kyrion**.*

fearing the Lord.

3:23a

ὃ ἐὰν ποιῆτε,

ho ean poiēte,

Whatever you do,

3:23b

ἐκ ψυχῆς ἐργάζεσθε,

*ek psy**chēs** erga**zesthe**,*

work with all your heart,

3:23c

ὡς τῷ κυρίῳ καὶ οὐκ ἀνθρώποις,

*hōs **tō** kyriō **kai** ouk an**thrō**pois,*

as to the Lord and not to people,

3:24a

εἰδότες ὅτι ἀπὸ κυρίου ἀπολήμψεσθε

eidotes hoti apo kyriou apolēmpsesthe

τὴν ἀνταπόδοσιν τῆς κληρονομίας·

tēn antapodosin tēs klēronomias;

**knowing that you will receive from the Lord
the inheritance as your reward;**

3:24b

τῷ κυρίῳ Χριστῷ δουλεύετε·

tō kyriō Christō douleuete;

you are serving the Lord Christ.

3:25a

ὁ γὰρ ἀδικῶν κομίσεται ὃ ἠδίκησεν,

ho gar adikōn komisetai ho ēdikēsen,

For whoever does wrong will be repaid for their wrongs,

3:25b

καὶ οὐκ ἔστιν προσωπολημψία.

kai ouk estin prosōpolēmpsia.

and there is no partiality.

4:1a

Οἱ κύριοι, τὸ δίκαιον καὶ τὴν ἰσότητα

Hoi kyrioi, to dikaion kai tēn isotēta

τοῖς δούλοις παρέχεσθε,

tois doulois parechesthe,

Masters, treat your slaves with justice and fairness,

4:1b

εἰδότες ὅτι καὶ ὑμεῖς ἔχετε κύριον ἐν οὐρανῷ.

eidotes hoti kai hymeis echete kyrion en ouranō.

knowing that you also have a Master in heaven.

Οἱ δοῦλοι, ὑπακούετε κατὰ πάντα
τοῖς κατὰ σάρκα κυρίοις,

Slaves, obey your earthly masters in everything,

Greek	English	Parsing	Type
Οἱ ὁ	the *Hoi*	NOM PL MASC	article
δοῦλοι δοῦλος	slaves *dou·loi*	NOM PL MASC	noun
ὑπακούετε ὑπακούω	(you all) obey *hyp·a·**kou**·e·te*	PRES ACT IMPV 2ND PL	verb
κατὰ κατά	according to *ka·**ta***	---	prep
πάντα πᾶς	all (things) ***pan**·ta*	ACC PL NEUT	adj
τοῖς ὁ	to the (ones) *tois*	DAT PL MASC	article
κατὰ κατά	according to *ka·**ta***	---	prep
σάρκα σάρξ	flesh *sar·ka*	ACC SG FEM	noun
κυρίοις κύριος	to masters *ky·**ri**·ois*	DAT PL MASC	noun

Paul transitions from the husband-wife and parent-child relationships to the slave-master relationship, which is the bulk of this section from 3:18 to 4:1. The fact that Paul uses **ὑπακούετε** ("obey") here, as he does for children in 3:20, again highlights the fact that the instruction Paul gave to wives in 3:18 was not for them to obey their husbands. Slaves as well as children, however, were expected to obey their masters and parents, respectively.

μὴ ἐν ὀφθαλμοδουλίαις,

not only when they are watching,

Greek	English	Parsing	Type
μὴ μή	not *mē*	---	particle
ἐν ἐν	with/by *en*	---	prep
ὀφθαλμοδουλίαις ὀφθαλμοδουλία	eye-service *o·phthal·mo·dou·li·ais*	DAT PL FEM	noun

ὡς ἀνθρωπάρεσκοι,			
as people pleasers,			
ὡς	as	---	adv
ὡς	*hōs*		
ἀνθρωπάρεσκοι	people-pleasing (ones)	NOM PL MASC	adj
ἀνθρωπάρεσκος	*an·thrō·**pa**·re·skoi*		

The only other use of this word is in Eph 6:6, a verse extremely similar to this one in Colossians. It literally means "people pleasing," but carries the connotation of doing so without regard to values or principles.

ἀλλ᾽ ἐν ἁπλότητι καρδίας,			
but with sincerity of heart,			
ἀλλ᾽	but	---	conj
ἀλλά	*all'*		
ἐν	in/by/with	---	prep
ἐν	*en*		
ἁπλότητι	sincerity	DAT SG FEM	noun
ἁπλότης	*ha·**plo**·tē·ti*		
καρδίας	of heart	GEN SG FEM	noun
καρδία	*kar·**di**·as*		

φοβούμενοι τὸν κύριον.			
fearing the Lord.			
φοβούμενοι	fearing	PRES MID PTCP	verb
φοβέω	*pho·**bou**·me·noi*	NOM PL MASC	
τὸν	the	ACC SG MASC	article
ὁ	***ton***		
κύριον	Lord	ACC SG MASC	noun
κύριος	***ky**·ri·on*		

An argument could be made that the "lord" (**κύριος**) to be feared is not the Lord God, but the earthly master, since Paul has just used this word **κύριος** to describe the slave owner at the beginning of this sentence. Nevertheless, and in agreement with most modern translations, translating it as "the Lord" makes the most sense, not least since Paul will return to this language in 3:23.

ὃ ἐὰν ποιῆτε,

Whatever you do,

ὃ	whatever	ACC SG NEUT	relative
ὅς	*ho*		pron
ἐὰν	if	---	cond
ἐάν	*e·an*		
ποιῆτε	(you all) might do	PRES ACT SUBJ	verb
ποιέω	*poi·ē·te*	2ND PL	

ἐκ ψυχῆς ἐργάζεσθε,

work with all your heart,

ἐκ	from	---	prep
ἐκ	*ek*		
ψυχῆς	soul	GEN SG FEM	noun
ψυχή	*psy·chēs*		
ἐργάζεσθε	(you all) work	PRES MID IMPV	verb
ἐργάζομαι	*er·ga·ze·sthe*	2ND PL	

ὡς τῷ κυρίῳ καὶ οὐκ ἀνθρώποις,

as to the Lord and not to people,

ὡς	as	---	adv
ὡς	*hōs*		
τῷ	to the	DAT SG MASC	article
ὁ	*tō*		
κυρίῳ	Lord	DAT SG MASC	noun
κύριος	*ky·ri·ō*		
καὶ	and	---	conj
καί	*kai*		
οὐκ	not	---	particle
οὐ	*ouk*		
ἀνθρώποις	people	DAT PL MASC	noun
ἄνθρωπος	*an·thrō·pois*		

**εἰδότες ὅτι ἀπὸ κυρίου ἀπολήμψεσθε
τὴν ἀνταπόδοσιν τῆς κληρονομίας·**

knowing that you will receive from the Lord
the inheritance as your reward;

εἰδότες	knowing	PERF ACT PTCP	verb
οἶδα	ei·**do**·tes	NOM PL MASC	
ὅτι	that	---	conj
ὅτι	**ho**·ti		
ἀπὸ	(away) from	---	prep
ἀπό	a·**po**		
κυρίου	Lord	GEN SG MASC	noun
κύριος	ky·**ri**·ou		
ἀπολήμψεσθε	(you all) will receive	FUT MID IND	verb
ἀπολαμβάνω	a·po·**lēm**·pse·sthe	2ND PL	
τὴν	the	ACC SG FEM	article
ὁ	**tēn**		
ἀνταπόδοσιν	reward	ACC SG FEM	noun
ἀνταπόδοσις	an·ta·**po**·do·sin		
τῆς	of the	GEN SG FEM	article
ὁ	**tēs**		
κληρονομίας	(of) inheritance	GEN SG FEM	noun
κληρονομία	klē·ro·no·**mi**·as		

The "inheritance" here is the same "inheritance" mentioned in 1:12—a participation in all the heavenly realities that come with participation in the kingdom of light, in contrast to participation in the kingdom of darkness.

τῷ κυρίῳ Χριστῷ δουλεύετε·

you are serving the Lord Christ.

τῷ	to the	DAT SG MASC	article
ὁ	**tō**		
κυρίῳ	Lord	DAT SG MASC	noun
κύριος	ky·**ri**·ō		
Χριστῷ	Christ	DAT SG MASC	noun
Χριστός	Chri·**stō**		
δουλεύετε	(you all) serve/slave	PRES ACT IND	verb
δουλεύω	dou·**leu**·e·te	2ND PL	

ὁ γὰρ ἀδικῶν κομίσεται ὃ ἠδίκησεν,

For whoever does wrong will be repaid for their wrongs,

Greek	Gloss	Parsing	Type
ὁ ὁ	the *ho*	NOM SG MASC	article
γὰρ γάρ	for *gar*	---	conj
ἀδικῶν ἀδικέω	(one) doing unjustly *a·di·kōn*	PRES ACT PTCP NOM SG MASC	verb
κομίσεται κομίζω	(he/she) will bring *ko·mi·se·tai*	FUT MID IND 3RD SG	verb
ὃ ὅς	which *ho*	ACC SG NEUT	relative pron
ἠδίκησεν ἀδικέω	(he/she) treated unjustly *ē·di·kē·sen*	AOR ACT IND 3RD SG	verb

The origin of this principle is likely that of *lex talionis* from Exod 21:23–25. More closely, though, Paul has already stated that the wrath of God will come to those who are disobedient in Col 3:6.

καὶ οὐκ ἔστιν προσωπολημψία.

and there is no partiality.

Greek	Gloss	Parsing	Type
καὶ καί	and *kai*	---	conj
οὐκ οὐ	not *ouk*	---	particle
ἔστιν εἰμί	(it) is *e·stin*	PRES ACT IND 3RD SG	verb
προσωπολημψία προσωπολημψία	favoritism *pro·sō·po·lēm·psi·a*	NOM SG FEM	noun

This theme of partiality or favoritism is also strongly emphasized in Rom 2. In Col 3:11 Paul has already declared that slave and free are both equal in Christ, and therefore both can anticipate judgment for wrongdoing. This statement also serves to connect Paul's discussion of the slave's behavior to that of the slave owner's behavior in the following verse.

Οἱ κύριοι, τὸ δίκαιον καὶ τὴν ἰσότητα
τοῖς δούλοις παρέχεσθε,

Masters, treat your slaves with justice and fairness,

Greek	English	Parsing 1	Parsing 2
Οἱ ὁ	the *Hoi*	NOM PL MASC	article
κύριοι κύριος	masters *ky·ri·oi*	NOM PL MASC	noun
τὸ ὁ	the *to*	ACC SG NEUT	article
δίκαιον δίκαιος	just *di·kai·on*	ACC SG NEUT	adj
καὶ καί	and *kai*	---	conj
τὴν ὁ	the *tēn*	ACC SG FEM	article
ἰσότητα ἰσότης	fairness *i·so·tē·ta*	ACC SG FEM	noun
τοῖς ὁ	to the *tois*	DAT PL MASC	article
δούλοις δοῦλος	slaves *dou·lois*	DAT PL MASC	noun
παρέχεσθε παρέχω	(you all) offer yourselves *par·e·che·sthe*	PRES MID IMPV 2ND PL	verb

Paul's use of the word **δίκαιος** ("just") is ubiquitous throughout his letters, yet **ἰσότης** ("fairness") is found only here and in 2 Cor 8:13–14. While in 2 Corinthians it means equality, here the nuance is likely one of fairness or of fair treatment within the social constructs of a master-slave relationship.

εἰδότες ὅτι καὶ ὑμεῖς ἔχετε κύριον ἐν οὐρανῷ.

knowing that you also have a Master in heaven.

Greek	English	Parsing 1	Parsing 2
εἰδότες οἶδα	knowing *ei·do·tes*	PERF ACT PTCP NOM PL MASC	verb
ὅτι ὅτι	that *ho·ti*	---	conj
καὶ καί	also *kai*	---	conj
ὑμεῖς σύ	you (all) *hy·meis*	2ND NOM PL	personal pron

ἔχετε ἔχω	(you all) have *e·che·te*	PRES ACT IND 2ND PL	verb
κύριον κύριος	Master *ky·ri·on*	ACC SG MASC	noun
ἐν ἐν	in *en*	---	prep
οὐρανῷ οὐρανός	heaven *ou·ra·nō*	DAT SG MASC	noun

Big Idea. Perhaps more than in other relationships, it is especially important to live lives worthy of the Lord with those in our own households.

 Bridge to Theology. God cares about how we interact with and relate to one another. Our relationships as those who are in Christ ought to reflect the relationship between Jesus and the Father. As with everything in our lives, they ought to be worthy of the Lord. There ought to be submission, love, patience, encouragement, support, and justice. The relationships listed here in Colossians are all relevant for today, except for the master-slave relationship. Perhaps some of these same principles can be applied in the modern-day workplace environment with its various hierarchical structures.

 Illustrations/Applications. Great care ought to be taken here in preaching on these texts, lest anything be communicated that is not clearly present in the text. Discussions regarding the kind of marriage relationship that may or may not be implicit in the text can be found in lengthier commentaries. For those looking for additional resources on how to make sense of this passage for our present day, I recommend two resources: Brian J. Walsh and Sylvia C. Keesmaat's *Colossians Remixed: Subverting the Empire* (2004), and Margaret Y. MacDonald's *The Power of Children: The Construction of Christian Families in the Greco-Roman World* (2014). Here, let us summarize by saying that what Paul is communicating is about living lives worthy of the Lord, established on the knowledge and wisdom found only in Christ, and rooted in the fruit of the spirit of Christ. This is expected of every party mentioned in this text. How this gets communicated within the sermon can take several forms, most of which would be not much different from the illustrations mentioned in the previous passage, "Vices and Virtues of Death and Life."

The relationship that receives the greatest amount of attention is the master-slave relationship. When we consider the overlaps between this relationship in the ancient world and today's modern work environment with its hierarchical structure, several specific illustrations can be made. First, you might challenge those in your congregation in positions of leadership to examine the ways in which they relate to their employees, how they actively support their career goals, whether they lead with justice and fairness, and whether they lead with a Christ-like humility. An apropos reminder here might be that God demonstrated his great power over evil through his self-sacrifice on the cross (2:15). Second, you can remind these parishioners who are in lower-level positions that it's perfectly fine to have and strive for career goals. At the end of the day, though, it is not their supervisors they should strive to impress, or the values of their supervisors (who may or may not be Christ followers) that should determine the shape of their work, but Christ himself and his values. For both the supervisor and the lower-level employee, these values should be a natural outflow of their new, risen identity in Christ, leading them all to "work for the Lord" (3:23) and not another human.

EXHORTATIONS AND GREETINGS

Paul concludes the letter with a final plea to remember him and Timothy and others in prayer, that they would have an effective ministry. He also challenges the Colossian Christians to practice wisdom when they interact with those who are not part of the kingdom of the Son, making the most of every opportunity. The letter concludes with a traditional list of greetings and salutations.

2a

Τῇ προσευχῇ προσκαρτερεῖτε,

Tē proseuchē proskartereite,

Devote yourselves to prayer,

2b

γρηγοροῦντες ἐν αὐτῇ ἐν εὐχαριστίᾳ,

grēgorountes en autē en eucharistia,

being watchful in it with thanksgiving,

3a

προσευχόμενοι ἅμα καὶ περὶ ἡμῶν,

proseuchomenoi hama kai peri hēmōn,

And pray for us, too,

3b

ἵνα ὁ θεὸς ἀνοίξῃ ἡμῖν θύραν τοῦ λόγου,

hina ho theos anoixē hēmin thyran tou logou,

that God may open a door for our message.

3c

λαλῆσαι τὸ μυστήριον τοῦ χριστοῦ,

lalēsai to mystērion tou christou,

That we may declare the mystery of Christ,

3d

δι᾽ ὃ καὶ δέδεμαι,

di᾽ ho kai dedemai,

on account of which I am in prison,

4a

ἵνα φανερώσω αὐτὸ

hina phanerōsō auto

that I might declare it clearly

4b

ὡς δεῖ μὲ λαλῆσαι.

hōs dei me lalēsai.

as I ought to.

5a

Ἐν σοφίᾳ περιπατεῖτε πρὸς τοὺς ἔξω,

*En sophia peripateite **pros tous** exō,*

Live lives of wisdom among outsiders,

5b

τὸν καιρὸν ἐξαγοραζόμενοι.

ton kairon exagorazomenoi.

making the most of every opportunity.

6a

ὁ λόγος ὑμῶν πάντοτε ἐν χάριτι,

ho logos hymōn pantote en chariti,

Let your conversations always be gracious,

6b

ἅλατι ἠρτυμένος,

halati ērtymenos,

seasoned with salt,

6c

εἰδέναι πῶς δεῖ ὑμᾶς ἑνὶ ἑκάστῳ ἀποκρίνεσθαι.

*eidenai **pōs dei** hymas heni hekastō apokrinesthai.*

so that you might know how you ought to answer everyone.

7–18   **[SUMMARIZED BELOW]**

2a	Τῇ προσευχῇ προσκαρτερεῖτε,		
	Devote yourselves to prayer,		
Τῇ	to the	DAT SG FEM	article
ὁ	*Tē*		
προσευχῇ	prayer	DAT SG FEM	noun
προσευχή	*pros·eu·chē*		
προσκαρτερεῖτε	(you all) continue	PRES ACT IMPV	verb
προσκαρτερέω	*pros·kar·te·rei·te*	2ND PL	

γρηγοροῦντες ἐν αὐτῇ ἐν εὐχαριστίᾳ,

being watchful in it with thanksgiving,

γρηγοροῦντες	watching	PRES ACT PTCP	verb
γρηγορέω	grē·go·**roun**·tes	NOM PL MASC	
ἐν	in	---	prep
ἐν	en		
αὐτῇ	it	DAT SG FEM	personal
αὐτός	au·**tē**		pron
ἐν	in/with	---	prep
ἐν	en		
εὐχαριστίᾳ	thanksgiving	DAT SG FEM	noun
εὐχαριστία	eu·cha·ri·**sti**·a		

προσευχόμενοι ἅμα καὶ περὶ ἡμῶν,

And pray for us, too,

προσευχόμενοι	praying	PRES MID PTCP	verb
προσεύχομαι	pros·eu·**cho**·me·noi	NOM PL MASC	
ἅμα	at the same time	---	adv
ἅμα	**ha**·ma		
καὶ	and/also/even	---	conj
καί	**kai**		
περὶ	about/concerning	---	prep
περί	pe·**ri**		
ἡμῶν	us	1ST GEN PL	personal
ἐγώ	hē·**mōn**		pron

ἵνα ὁ θεὸς ἀνοίξῃ ἡμῖν θύραν τοῦ λόγου,

that God may open a door for our message.

ἵνα	that	---	conj
ἵνα	**hi**·na		
ὁ	the	NOM SG MASC	article
ὁ	ho		
θεὸς	God	NOM SG MASC	noun
θεός	the·**os**		
ἀνοίξῃ	(he) might open	AOR ACT SUBJ	verb
ἀνοίγω	an·**oi**·xē	3RD SG	
ἡμῖν	to us	1ST DAT PL	personal
ἐγώ	hē·**min**		pron

θύραν	door	ACC SG FEM	noun
θύρα	*thy·ran*		
τοῦ	of the	GEN SG MASC	article
ὁ	*tou*		
λόγου	(of) word	GEN SG MASC	noun
λόγος	*lo·gou*		

3c	λαλῆσαι τὸ μυστήριον τοῦ χριστοῦ,		
	That we may declare the mystery of Christ,		

λαλῆσαι	to speak	AOR ACT INF	verb
λαλέω	*la·lē·sai*		
τὸ	the	ACC SG NEUT	article
ὁ	*to*		
μυστήριον	mystery	ACC SG NEUT	noun
μυστήριον	*my·stē·ri·on*		
τοῦ	of the	GEN SG MASC	article
ὁ	*tou*		
χριστοῦ	(of) Christ	GEN SG MASC	noun
Χριστός	*chri·stou*		

Τοῦ χριστοῦ ("of Christ") is an epexegetical genitive: Christ is the mystery. See Col 2:2.

3d	δι᾽ ὃ καὶ δέδεμαι,		
	on account of which I am in prison,		

δι᾽	on account of	---	prep
διά	*di'*		
ὃ	which	ACC SG NEUT	relative
ὅς	*ho*		pron
καὶ	also/even	---	conj
καί	*kai*		
δέδεμαι	I have been bound	PERF PASS IND	verb
δέω	*de·de·mai*	1ST SG	

4a

ἵνα φανερώσω αὐτὸ

that I might declare it clearly

ἵνα ἵνα	that/in order that *hi·na*	---	conj
φανερώσω φανερόω	I might show *pha·ne·rō·sō*	AOR ACT SUBJ 1ST SG	verb
αὐτὸ αὐτός	it *au·to*	ACC SG NEUT	personal pron

4b

ὡς δεῖ μὲ λαλῆσαι.

as I ought to.

ὡς ὡς	as *hōs*	---	adv
δεῖ δεῖ	it is necessary *dei*	PRES ACT IND 3RD SG	verb
μὲ ἐγώ	me *me*	1ST ACC SG	personal pron
λαλῆσαι λαλέω	to speak *la·lē·sai*	AOR ACT INF	verb

5a

Ἐν σοφίᾳ περιπατεῖτε πρὸς τοὺς ἔξω,

Live lives of wisdom among outsiders,

Ἐν ἐν	in *En*	---	prep
σοφίᾳ σοφία	wisdom *so·phi·a*	DAT SG FEM	noun
περιπατεῖτε περιπατέω	(you all) walk *pe·ri·pa·tei·te*	PRES ACT IMPV 2ND PL	verb
πρὸς πρός	with/toward *pros*	---	prep
τοὺς ὁ	the (ones) *tous*	ACC PL MASC	article
ἔξω ἔξω	outside *e·xō*	---	adv

Here is the fourth and final time **περιπατέω** ("to walk") is used in Colossians (also 1:10; 2:6; 3:7), again in an exhortation to the Colossians that they would live lives of godly wisdom, lives worthy of the gospel of Christ.

τὸν καιρὸν ἐξαγοραζόμενοι.

making the most of every opportunity.

τὸν	the	ACC SG MASC	article
ὁ	*ton*		
καιρὸν	opportunity/time	ACC SG MASC	noun
καιρός	*kai·**ron***		
ἐξαγοραζόμενοι	redeeming/making the most of	PRES MID PTCP NOM PL MASC	verb
ἐξαγοράζω	*ex·a·go·ra·**zo**·me·noi*		

ὁ λόγος ὑμῶν πάντοτε ἐν χάριτι,

Let your conversations always be gracious,

ὁ	the	NOM SG MASC	article
ὁ	*ho*		
λόγος	word/speech	NOM SG MASC	noun
λόγος	*lo·gos*		
ὑμῶν	of you (all)/your	2ND GEN PL	personal pron
σύ	*hy·**mōn***		
πάντοτε	always	---	adv
πάντοτε	*pan·to·te*		
ἐν	in/by/with	---	prep
ἐν	*en*		
χάριτι	grace	DAT SG FEM	noun
χάρις	*cha·ri·ti*		

ἄλατι ἠρτυμένος,

seasoned with salt,

ἄλατι	salt	DAT SG NEUT	noun
ἅλας	*ha·la·ti*		
ἠρτυμένος	(one) having been seasoned with	PERF PASS PTCP NOM SG MASC	verb
ἀρτύω	*ēr·ty·me·nos*		

A conversation that is "seasoned with salt" is one that is refined, tactful, and, primarily—as Paul said in the previous clause—"gracious."

6c	**εἰδέναι πῶς δεῖ ὑμᾶς ἑνὶ ἑκάστῳ ἀποκρίνεσθαι.**

so that you might know how you ought to answer everyone.

εἰδέναι οἶδα	to know *ei·de·nai*	PERF ACT INF	verb
πῶς πῶς	how *pōs*	---	adv
δεῖ δεῖ	it is necessary *dei*	PRES ACT IND 3RD SG	verb
ὑμᾶς σύ	you (all) *hy·mas*	2ND ACC PL	personal pron
ἑνὶ εἷς	to one *he·ni*	DAT SG MASC	adj
ἑκάστῳ ἕκαστος	to each *he·ka·stō*	DAT SG MASC	adj
ἀποκρίνεσθαι ἀποκρίνομαι	to answer *a·po·kri·ne·sthai*	PRES MID INF	verb

4:7–18	**SUMMARY**

Paul concludes the epistle with a closing salutation, which was typical in first-century letters. He says that he is sending the letter with Tychicus and Onesimus, who will share an update on Paul's ministry with the Colossians, and then he offers final greetings to the Colossians from those who are with him, including Aristarchus, Mark, Justus, Epaphras, Luke, and Demas.

From Text to Sermon

 Big Idea. Proclaim the gospel with wisdom and grace.

 Bridge to Theology. Paul's final words before he turns to his list of greetings is about the proclamation of the gospel. He asks the Colossians to pray for him and for his proclamation of the gospel—the reason he is in prison in the first place. And he tells the Colossians to be aware of how they share the gospel with "outsiders" (4:5), likely those in Colossae who are not part of the church. When they have exchanges with them, their words and actions ought to be filled with wisdom and grace. In doing so, Christ will be proclaimed.

 Illustrations/Applications. This is an ideal opportunity to encourage your listeners to think about their relationships with non-Christians. Perhaps you can challenge them to think about what makes their lives noticeably different from those of the "outsiders" in their spheres. In what way are they proclaiming the gospel of Christ through their lives?

Additionally, here is a wonderful opportunity to explore exactly what gospel we are believing and proclaiming. For example, we know that people are less inclined to be concerned about something called "sin" in our post-Christian, Western culture than they might have been in a predominantly Christian or religious culture. If, then, the gospel we proclaim to the "outsiders" in our midst is purely a gospel of forgiveness of sin, it may well fall on deaf ears. But what if the gospel we proclaim has something to say to the non-Christian going through a divorce or who is recently diagnosed with cancer or who can't seem to get pregnant or who has repeat miscarriages? What does our version of the gospel have to say to the person who can't seem to find success in the workplace or can't find a spouse or who is differently abled? Or, in a different vein, what does our version of the gospel have to say to the person who experiences sexism or racism? These are the interactions that could use a bit of salt seasoning (4:6). If the gospel we proclaim doesn't have something to say to each of these circumstances, then it's not the whole gospel. These are the people who need to hear that, yes, Jesus's death offers us forgiveness, but also that Jesus is the creator of a good creation, is Lord over that same, now-broken creation, has defeated evil through his divine sacrifice, and is making *all things* new, restoring and reconciling *all things* back to himself. This is a gospel that preaches. This is a gospel that "outsiders" want to hear and need to hear. This is the gospel that Colossians reminds us of. The remarkable thing is that this gospel isn't something new; it's woven throughout the biblical narrative. We just need to read, preach, and teach Colossians a bit more frequently!

WORKS CITED

Bird, Michael F. 2009. *Colossians, Philemon.* New Covenant Commentary Series. Eugene: Cascade.

Davies, J. P. 2023. "Apocalyptic Paul." Pages 24–34 in *Dictionary of Paul and His Letters.* 2nd ed. Edited by Scot McKnight. Downers Grove: IVP Academic.

Gorman, M. J. 2023. "In Christ." Pages 476–82 in *Dictionary of Paul and His Letters.* 2nd ed. Edited by Scot McKnight. Downers Grove: IVP Academic.

Gupta, Nijay K. 2013. *Colossians: Smyth & Helwys Bible Commentary.* Macon: Smyth & Helwys.

MacDonald, Margaret Y. 2014. *The Power of Children: The Construction of Christian Families in the Greco-Roman World.* Waco: Baylor.

McKnight, Scot. 2018. *The Letter to the Colossians.* New International Commentary on the New Testament. Grand Rapids: Eerdmans.

Walsh, Brian J. and Sylvia C. Keesmaat. 2004. *Colossians Remixed: Subverting the Empire.* Downers Grove: IVP Academic.

Westfall, Cynthia Long. 2016. *Paul and Gender: Reclaiming the Apostle's Vision for Men and Women in Christ.* Grand Rapids: Baker.

TEXT-CRITICAL NOTES

For those who wish to incorporate textual criticism into their preparation of the Greek text of the passages discussed in this volume, the following apparatus lists exegetically significant text-critical variations that exist among the Westcott-Hort text ("WH"), which is the basis for the Greek text of Colossians found in this book, and the 27th edition of the Nestle-Aland text ("NA") and the Robinson-Pierpont Byzantine text ("RP"). These data are reproduced, with permission, from the comparative apparatus of an edition of the Westcott-Hort text published by Hendrickson under the title *The Greek New Testament*.[1]

Any readings listed below that the author has chosen to incorporate into the Greek text found in the present volume are set in **bold** type.

Colossians 1:1–14 (excluding vv. 3–8, which are summarized in this volume)

1	WH: Χριστοῦ Ἰησοῦ RP: Ἰησοῦ χριστοῦ
2	RP: *add* καὶ κυρίου Ἰησοῦ χριστοῦ *after* ἡμῶν
10	RP: *add* ὑμᾶς *after* περιπατῆσαι
	WH: τῇ ἐπιγνώσει RP: εἰς τὴν ἐπίγνωσιν
11	WH: μακροθυμίαν μετὰ χαρᾶς,
	ΝΑ: μακροθυμίαν. Μετὰ χαρᾶς
12	{WH}: *add* θεῷ *before* πατρὶ
	WH: ὑμᾶς {WH}/RP: ἡμᾶς

---

1. B. F. Westcott and F. J. A. Hort, *The Greek New Testament, with Expanded Dictionary* (Peabody, MA: Hendrickson Publishers, 2008), which is based on the 1885 edition of the Westcott-Hort text. "WH" represents the text printed in the aforecited volume; "NA" represents the text printed in Barbara Aland, Kurt Aland, Johannes Karavidopoulos, Carlo M. Martini, and Bruce M. Metzger, eds., *Novum Testamentum Graece*, 27th ed. (Stuttgart: Deutsche Bibelgesellschaft, 1993); and "RP" represents the text printed in Maurice Robinson and William G. Pierpont, eds., *The New Testament in the Original Greek: Byzantine Textform* (Southborough, MA: Chilton Book Publishing, 2005). The abbreviation "{WH}" denotes marginal readings in the Westcott-Hort text, and the use of brackets around an edition abbreviation (e.g., "[NA]") indicates that the reading listed is found in brackets in the text in question. For more details, see pp. xxi–xxvii of the 2008 Hendrickson version of *The Greek New Testament* cited at the beginning of this note, esp. p. xxvi, which further explains which kinds of (exegetically significant) variations are included here and which kinds of (exegetically insignificant) variations are omitted.

13	WH: ἐρύσατο NA/RP: ἐρρύσατο
14	WH: ἔχομεν {WH}: ἔσχομεν

Colossians 1:15-23

16	RP: *add* τὰ *before (second occurrence of)* ἐν
	RP: *add* τὰ *before* ἐπὶ
18	**NA/RP: *omit* [ἡ] *before* ἀρχή**
20	WH: [δι᾽ αὐτοῦ] RP: δι᾽ αὐτοῦ
	WH: ἐν RP: ἐπὶ
21-22	RP: *end v. 21 after* ἀποκατήλλαξεν
22	WH: ἀποκατήλλαξεν {WH}: ἀποκατηλλάγητε
23	WH: εἴ γε RP: εἴγε
	RP: *add* τῇ *before* κτίσει

Colossians 1:24-2:5

1:26	WH: νῦν RP: νυνὶ
1:27	WH: ὅ {WH}/RP: ὅς
1:28	RP: *add* Ἰησοῦ *after* χριστῷ
2:1	WH: ὑπὲρ RP: περὶ
	WH: ἑόρακαν RP: ἑωράκασιν
2:2	WH: συνβιβασθέντες RP: συμβιβασθέντων
	WH: πᾶν πλοῦτος RP: πάντα πλοῦτον
	RP: *add* καὶ πατρὸς καὶ τοῦ *after* θεοῦ
2:3	RP: *add* τῆς *before* γνώσεως
2:4	RP: *add* δὲ *after* Τοῦτο
	WH: μηδεὶς RP: μή τις

Colossians 2:6-15

7	RP: *add* ἐν *before* τῇ
	WH: περισσεύοντες [ἐν αὐτῇ] **NA: περισσεύοντες**
	RP: περισσεύοντες ἐν αὐτῇ
8	WH: ὑμᾶς ἔσται {WH}: ἔσται ὑμᾶς
11	RP: *add* τῶν ἁμαρτιῶν *before* τῆς σαρκός
12	WH: βαπτίσματι NA: βαπτισμῷ
	RP: *add* τῶν *before* νεκρῶν
13	[NA]/RP: *add* ἐν *before* τοῖς

WH: *(second occurrence of)* ὑμᾶς   {WH}: ἡμᾶς

13–14   **WH: αὐτῷ· χαρισάμενος ἡμῖν . . . ἡμῖν,**
        {WH}: αὐτῷ, χαρισάμενος ἡμῖν . . . ἡμῖν·
        NA: αὐτῷ, χαρισάμενος ἡμῖν . . . ἡμῖν,

Colossians 2:16–23

16   WH: καὶ   {WH}/RP: ἢ
      WH: νεομηνίας   RP: νουμηνίας
17   WH: ἅ   {WH}: ὅ
      RP: *omit* τοῦ *before* χριστοῦ
18   {WH}: *θέλων . . . ἐμβατεύων*
      WH: ἑόρακεν   RP: μὴ ἑώρακεν
20   WH: δογματίζεσθε   NA: δογματίζεσθε;   **RP: δογματίζεσθε,**
23   WH: [καὶ]   RP: καὶ
      {WH}: *[καὶ] . . . σαρκός*

Colossians 3:1–11

4   WH: ἡμῶν   **{WH}/NA: ὑμῶν**
5   RP: *add* ὑμῶν *after* μέλη
6   [NA]/RP: *add* ἐπὶ τοὺς υἱοὺς τῆς ἀπειθείας *after* θεοῦ
7   WH: τούτοις   RP: αὐτοῖς
11   [NA]/RP: *add* τὰ *before* πάντα

Colossians 3:12–17

12   WH: ἅγιοι καὶ   {WH}: ἅγιοι,
      WH: πραΰτητα   RP: πραότητα
13   WH: κύριος   {WH}/RP: χριστὸς
14   WH: ὅ   RP: ἥτις
15   WH: χριστοῦ   RP: θεοῦ
      WH: [ἑνὶ]   **NA/RP: ἑνὶ**
16   WH: χριστοῦ   {WH}: κυρίου
      WH: πλουσίως   **NA: πλουσίως,**
      WH: σοφίᾳ·   **NA: σοφίᾳ,**
      WH: ἑαυτοὺς   **NA: ἑαυτοὺς,**
      WH: ὕμνοις,   RP: καὶ ὕμνοις, καὶ
      {WH}/[NA]: *add* τῇ *before* χάριτι

WH: ταῖς καρδίαις   RP: τῇ καρδίᾳ

WH: θεῷ   RP: κυρίῳ

17   WH: ὅτι ἐάν   **NA: ὅ τι ἐάν**   RP: ὅ τι ἄν

RP: *add* καὶ *after* θεῷ

Colossians 3:18–4:1

3:18   RP: *add* ἰδίοις *before* ἀνδράσιν

3:20   WH: εὐάρεστόν ἐστιν   RP: ἐστιν εὐάρεστόν

3:22   WH: ὀφθαλμοδουλίαις   {WH}/NA: ὀφθαλμοδουλίᾳ

WH: κύριον   RP: θεόν

3:23   WH: ὅ   RP: καὶ πᾶν ὅ τι

3:24   WH: ἀπολήμψεσθε   RP: λήψεσθε

RP: *add* γὰρ *after* τῷ

3:25   WH: γὰρ   RP: δὲ

WH: κομίσεται   RP: κομιεῖται

4:1   WH: οὐρανῷ   RP: οὐρανοῖς

INDEX OF BIBLICAL REFERENCES

NOTE: The primary purpose of a Scripture index in a book like this, where biblical passages are being treated directly, is not to present the reader with every biblical reference found in the book, but to offer ones that lie outside the range of each of the passages treated. Hence, this index presents references to such outside passages, plus verses from the passages treated in this book *but only when these are cross-referenced in a discussion of another verse found in these passages.*

ABOUT THE AUTHOR

HALEY JACOB (PhD, University of St Andrews) is Associate Professor and Chair of Theology at Whitworth University in Spokane, Washington, where she teaches courses that focus on biblical theology and Paul's epistles. After growing up in rural Minnesota, she earned MAs in Theology and New Testament at Gordon-Conwell Theological Seminary. She is the author of *Conformed to the Image of His Son: Reconsidering Paul's Theology of Glory in Romans*. She is married to Alan and has two young children, Phoebe and Brooks. In the last four years, she's learned how to keep both children and a garden alive. One has proven more difficult than the other!